Government and Politics
in the Twentieth Century

GOVERNMENT AND POLITICS
IN THE TWENTIETH CENTURY

by Gwendolen M. Carter

and John H. Herz

FREDERICK A. PRAEGER, *Publisher*
New York

BOOKS THAT MATTER

Published in the United States of America in 1961
by Frederick A. Praeger, Inc., Publisher
64 University Place, New York 3, N. Y.

Second Printing, 1962

All rights reserved

© Frederick A. Praeger, Inc., 1961

Library of Congress catalog card number 61-9661

GOVERNMENT AND POLITICS IN THE TWENTIETH CENTURY
is published in two editions:

   A paperback edition (U-504)
   A clothbound edition

Portions of this book have been adapted,
and some short passages reprinted,
with permission from the concluding section,
Part V, of *Major Foreign Powers,* 3rd edition,
© 1957 by Harcourt, Brace & World, Inc.

Manufactured in the United States of America

CONTENTS

	Introduction	*1*
I	*The Role of Government in Contemporary Society*	*3*
	The Rise of the Modern State 4	
	Big and Active Government 6	
II	*Democracy Versus Totalitarianism*	*9*
	Characteristics of Democracies 10	
	The Nature of Totalitarianism 12	
	Developing States Between Democracy and Totalitarianism 16	
	Is Democracy Adequate for Modern Conditions? 18	
III	*Patterns of Government*	*22*
	The One-Party Dictatorship 22	
	The Parliamentary Pattern 24	
	How Deep Does Western Influence Go? 46	
	The Extent of Diversity 51	
	The Trend Toward Uniformity 53	
IV	*The Framework of Limited Government*	*56*
	Origins and Functions of Constitutions 56	
	Basic Rights and Liberties Today 59	
	Constitutional Jurisdiction 68	
	Independence of the Judiciary 73	
	Deconcentration of Power 80	
V	*Channels of Political Action: Elections, Political Parties, and Legislatures*	*91*
	The Process and Purpose of Elections 92	
	Political Parties 99	
	Legislatures 125	

VI Political Leadership and Administration 132

The Headship of the State:
  The Leader "Reigns" 133
The Headship of the Government:
  The Leader "Rules" 135
Problems of Selection, Responsibility, and
  Succession of the Chief Executive 139
The Role and Selection of the
  Bureaucracy 148
Informal Channels of Access to the
  Leader 158
The Role of Pressure Groups 159

VII Belief Systems and Politics 165

The Role of Ideology 165
Church and State 171
The Liberal and the Totalitarian Polity 180

VIII The Interrelations of National and International Politics 183

From Self-Sufficiency to
  Interdependence 184
The Impact of Bipolarity 186
The Impact of International
  Organization 200

IX Democracy in the Modern World 205

The Two Patterns of Democracy and
  Dictatorship 206
Can Democracy Work? 209

Selected Bibliography 217

INTRODUCTION

The systematic study of comparative government and politics has commonly been concerned only with the institutions and activities of European countries and the United States. Moreover, in the still relatively rare works in which the institutions of the newer countries have been examined analytically, the consideration has nearly always been either of a particular state or of several of these states compared with each other. This book seeks to broaden the focus of comparative analysis by dealing with both developed and developing countries and by testing generalizations obtained from the study of mature states in the light of the experience of the newer states of Asia, Africa, the Middle East, and Latin America.

Accepting the dichotomy of democracy and totalitarianism, we recognize that even highly developed states do not conform exactly to the characteristic features of either system. Particularly among the newer states there are political systems which lie between democracy and totalitarianism, not only partaking of the characteristics of both, but also adding something distinctive of their own.

This book makes no pretense at finality. Rather, we have sought to stimulate further investigation into a field which becomes increasingly suggestive as its focus is widened. We have therefore deliberately sought great breadth of scope. We have been concerned with the operation and results in different settings of what may seem to be similar institutions, with those forces which make for uniformity and those which make for diversity, with the interaction of traditional and revolutionary forces, and with reactions to the strains of ideological conflict and cold war. While putting into sharp focus the divergencies of governmental and political systems in the twentieth-century world, and while not playing down the conflict situations which such divergency is bound to create, we hope also to have made clear the merit which can exist in systems that differ from Western democracy. It is in accordance with the democratic approach, whose validity we affirm, to grant others their right to find their own institutional answers to their particular problems. Only thus can this "one world" become a world of neighbors.

GWENDOLEN M. CARTER
JOHN H. HERZ

I

THE ROLE OF GOVERNMENT IN CONTEMPORARY SOCIETY

The author of the first great treatise on government and politics known to history found it necessary to analyze, compare, and contrast over one hundred and fifty polities and their constitutions as a basis for his conclusions. A present-day Aristotle would need to do at least as much to speak with any hope of realism of government and politics in the twentieth-century world. Compared with the range of political systems in the relatively close world of the ancient polis, that of current political units all over the world seems, indeed, to be vastly broader. Its diversity becomes apparent not only when one contrasts systems in the so-called "free" world with those of totalitarian dictatorships; there is, in addition, the heritage of "pre-modern" countries and their political ways of life. The liquidation of this heritage is on the agenda of our times, but it still affects the internal affairs of the areas concerned. It affects, too, their interrelations with longer-established states, as is attested by the sometimes promising, sometimes tragic story of their entrance as independent units into the modern world.

This entrance is as inevitable as it is relentless. Moreover, in addition, and in contrast to the diversity which results, there is the modern trend toward uniformity, especially in terms of the role and function of government in society. It is this trend which is the object of our initial analysis.

The distinguishing feature of modern government is its universal recognition and acceptance as an active force in the forming of economic and social conditions. In the United States, there remains a much greater attachment than in Great Britain or in France to the idea that government should be only an umpire adjudicating the rules by which other forces in society compete, but even there such governmental activities as the TVA or credit controls to prevent economic fluctuation are now accepted with little question. Thus, in the older democracies, and still more in the newer developing states as well as in Communist-controlled countries, government is looked on as a major, or even the dominant, organizing power in society.

THE RISE OF THE MODERN STATE

So much have we become accustomed to the idea of government as an active, positive agent in the direction of the affairs of our communities that we often fail to realize the significance of the change this idea represents. In the English-speaking countries particularly, the nineteenth-century view was that government should restrict itself to the basic, and somewhat negative, function of maintaining law and order, acting only, as the half-contemptuous phrase expresses it, as a "night watchman." The transformation of this concept of the state into the modern concept of the welfare or social-service state is indeed a revolution.

This transformation in the role of the state is in essence a by-product of economic and social changes which are themselves of revolutionary character. The French Revolution and the industrial revolution—two separate but nevertheless inescapably interrelated historical forces—gave rise to a profound change in attitudes toward the individual and his place within the community. The French Revolution preached the equality of individuals, a doctrine which directly challenged the long-existent, rigid social hierarchies of Europe; at the same time, it aroused the sentiment of nationalism which exalts the community. Thus, the individual was freed, only to be merged into the group. But if the French Revolution provided much of the ideology and spur for social change, it was the industrial revolution which provided the new circumstances in which change was inevitable. Industrialism, with its new modes of production, opened the way for individual activity and permitted social mobility to a degree never before seen. Yet, while industrialism stimulated individualism, particularly in its early stages, its own inner logic was toward mass production, standardization, and vast economic units. Thus with industrialization as with the French Revolution, the tendency was to free the individual from the restrictions of the past only to fit him into new and larger entities. Inevitably, the breakdown of traditional social and economic groupings produced the mass society characteristic of our time. In this mass society, the equalitarian drive stimulated change, while large-scale economic activity, coupled with tremendous population increases, tended to promote a new social stratification.

BIG AND ACTIVE GOVERNMENT

In this new mass society, the role of government—the complex of institutions that have a monopoly of organized force in internal and external affairs—of necessity has changed. The state, the organized political community, needs a certain degree of stability in the social system in order to maintain its own equilibrium; this requires not only the adjustment of conflicting demands by different groups in the new social and economic order, but also the deliberate creation of conditions of social well-being demanded by the new doctrine of equality. Thus, government, as the agent of the state, has been forced more and more to assume positive responsibility for the creation and distribution of wealth. In so doing, it has almost universally become big government, both in scope and in the numbers of those employed in carrying on its responsibilities.

There are two chief problems arising from this development. In the first place, a greatly increased number of persons become government officials and, thus, peculiarly subject to the pressures of an unscrupulous regime. In some Western countries, the state pays the salaries not only of those carrying on the public administration at the local as well as national level, but also of all those engaged in public education and even, as with the Evangelical Church in Germany, of the clergy. Democratic countries erect safeguards, such as merit and classification systems, and in France the highly effective Council of State, to protect public employees against favoritism in appointment and promotions, undue influence, or exploitation. It was not difficult, however, for the Hitler regime (to take but one example) to disregard many of these protective devices and use to the full the influence afforded by the unusually large number of public employees in Germany.

More serious, under normal conditions, is the problem of concentration of power, particularly power over the economy in a highly developed state. The struggle to improve living conditions has led all advanced states to undertake a substantial amount of public regulation of the economy and an increasing degree of economic planning. It is often argued that to subject the expert planners to control by the inexpert public would destroy the value of their plans. Moreover, planning requires a firm and stable government, it is said, for no plan can be effective if its sponsors are likely to be turned out of office at any moment and their policies reversed, or even if important modifications can be made by parliamentary vote. And while it is not difficult to point out that, in practice, democracies have erected safeguards in this field, too, such as decentralization through the public corporation, the very complexity and far-reaching character of the operations which government now undertakes can leave no one feeling entirely complacent about the degree to which popular control of public activities is possible.

In other words, to keep government in the twentieth-century world responsible and yet effective places a tremendous strain both on the machinery and the personnel of government as well as on the alertness and activity of the public and its organs of information. From this fact, some observers have drawn the conclusion that an authoritarian government, able to act promptly and decisively without regard to special pressures, constitutional obstacles, or the need to conciliate mass opinion, is far more efficient and far better suited to the conditions of modern government than is a democracy. We can point out in return that in two world wars, democracies proved able to mobilize their resources as efficiently, if not quite as quickly, as dictatorships, and that the more mature democracies have been able to provide higher standards of living for their people than have any dictatorships, though this is partly because of the richness of their resources and their advantage in having started earlier. But as we watch the progressive industrialization of the newer countries, we must be aware that one of their greatest difficulties will be so to handle their administrative machinery that it performs expertly the tasks which they ask of it and, at the same time, remains responsible and responsive to the interests of the public which it serves.

II

DEMOCRACY VERSUS TOTALITARIANISM

Although all modern governments today exercise a wide range of responsibilities, there remain highly significant differences between the objectives and techniques of those states which we call democratic and those which are avowedly totalitarian, whether of the Communist or fascist type. Democracy and totalitarianism as systems form polar points on the spectrum of political alternatives. At the same time, there is a wide variety of governmental forms between the two which do not fit neatly into either category. Moreover, totalitarian states differ in character not only between countries and between stages of development and of revolutionary fervor, but also in relation to their leaders: e.g., Khrushchev's program for the Soviet Union is more like that of Lenin than that of Stalin, while Stalin's regime bore strong resemblances to Hitler's Germany both in its statism and its personalization of leadership. On the other hand, even mature democracies sometimes exhibit, particularly in periods of crisis, some of the characteristics of totalitarianism. Nonetheless, there are clearly definable features of democracy and of totalitarianism which can be identified and used as standards for testing the character and operations of governmental systems. These differences are not only institutional but appear also in basic attitudes.

CHARACTERISTICS OF DEMOCRACIES

Democracies are characterized institutionally by limitations on governmental action to provide safeguards for individuals and groups, by means for securing the regular, periodic, and peaceful change of their leaders, and by organs of effective popular representation. In attitude, they require tolerance for opposing opinions, flexibility, and willingness for experimentation. Limitation on governmental actions means not only that there are private spheres of life in which government must not interfere, but also that governmental agents, like private persons, must abide by the rules of law and exercise authority only to the degree the law provides. Peaceful changes of representation and of leaders involve a system of elections with some genuine measure of choice between candidates, either at the nomination or the election level. It implies a system of nomination and also a formulation of program which is associated with the candidates who are running for office. It necessitates political organization, commonly in the form of political parties, to keep constant contact between the public and its leaders and representatives. Moreover, so that choice may be exercised freely and public policies kept under review, political parties and other associations must have the oppportunity openly to analyze issues, criticize governmental actions, and crystallize public sentiment. Organs of opinion—the press, radio, and TV—must be permitted the independent purveyance of news and formulation of judgments. Thus, freedom of speech, of association, and of assembly are essential political as well as civil rights.

To make democracy effective, however, requires not only institutions and guarantees, but also attitudes. Respect for the right of the people to assert their point of view, however unpopular or seemingly wrong-headed, is fundamental to the workings of the democratic process of discussion and choice. This basic attitude is expressed in the saying, "I abhor your opinion, but I shall fight to the death for your right to express it." Nothing can exert a greater influence on the democratic character of a state than the individual citizen's tolerance of (though not indifference to) ideas, whether expressed individually or through associations which are contrary to or challenge his own. Censorship and governmental restraint are obvious ways of creating conformism, but social pressure may be no less a force in crushing the interplay of ideas on which democracy depends.

Democracy is characterized further by respect for minority and individual rights, by the use of discussion rather than force to settle disputes, by an acceptance of the legitimacy of the system under which the people are governed, and by the experimental method. Democracies have ideals and objectives, but they do not have fixed goals. Thus they proceed through trial and error, changing their programs in response to popular need and present circumstance. All states are limited by their past and by their environment, but democracies believe that they are not restricted by any inevitable process of history and that there exist opportunities for experiment and choice of alternatives.

THE NATURE OF TOTALITARIANISM

In contrast to the conscious efforts of democracies to maintain diversity, open discussion, freedom of choice among ideas and leaders, and open-mindedness on future programs, totalitarianism is characterized by a persistent drive to enforce unity, by the crushing of open opposition, and by a leadership which claims superior, if not infallible knowledge of how policy should be directed and which exercises power through a self-perpetuating elite. Behind these actions lies an ideology, or doctrine, which justifies the concentration of power—and whatever restrictions on individual and group liberties this involves—as the means necessary to attain some ultimate and fixed goal or certain end toward which nature or history are said to strive.

Thus, totalitarian Communism, for instance, not only as seen from outside but even more in its self-interpretation, is very different from simple rule by force or autocracy. Because everything which happens now is meant to be merely a transitional stage on history's inexorable path toward a future depicted as one of complete human emancipation and freedom, everything, be it ever so coercive, partakes of the nature of a necessary but minor evil to attain this end. Opinion has to be controlled and censorship instituted; but this is only because portions of the public are still "backward" in their "social consciousness," and therefore have to be "educated" by a "vanguard" which possesses full consciousness of history and the things to come. This same vanguard has to exercise controls and accumulate powers which, to the uninitiated, look excessive and dictatorial; but the holders of power consider themselves the agents of a movement which fulfills the deepest yearnings of the masses of the people, and, therefore purport to act "democratically" in a more profound way than do the people's representatives in the West who, according to this view, are mere self-seeking agents or stooges of business and other "interests."

CONTRAST WITH AUTOCRACY

Thus, Communist leaders, in their own view, are performing the historic task of social and general reconstruction, a task which ennobles whatever shortcomings the current Eastern-style "democracies" may still embody. If East Berlin, for instance, appears shoddy to a Western visitor who contrasts it to the Western part of the city, it does not seem so to a person steeped in the "right" philosophy; to the latter, any building or enterprise owned "by the people" is intrinsically superior to the glittering façade of a structure which, because capitalist-owned, symbolizes the degeneracy of the capitalist system. Moreover, the former is bound, in due course, to surpass the latter, even in aesthetic terms, and thus will attain the beauty of the "higher system" which the true believer already discerns in what is defective at present.

Keeping in mind this kind of totalitarian self-interpretation, it is possible to differentiate between totalitarianism as a system aiming at the total transformation of life and society and claiming a total mandate for this purpose, and authoritarianism, or oligarchism, or autocracy—whichever term may be preferred—as being a system and regime which strives to maintain control in a community without basically changing its structure. This latter system, in contrast to totalitarianism, tends to preserve the traditional social structure and to work through established lines of authority. If the latter are effective, autocracy may be comparable to the indirect rule characteristic of early British colonial control in African territories which possessed strong tribal structures of authority. As a means of maintaining their dominance, authoritarian rulers commonly aim at preserving a climate of internal tranquility. While it is perhaps going too far to speak of General Charles de Gaulle's administration in the Fifth French Republic as a new-fashioned autocracy, its aim has been to reduce tensions, prevent social revolution, and establish governmental stability, all of which are normal objectives of an autocracy.

A totalitarian regime, such as a Communist-controlled one, unlike autocracy, makes rapid social change a major objective and mobilizes the instruments of the modern industrialized state—technology, education, communication media—to accelerate this process. The reasons are twofold: to move as rapidly as possible toward the transcendent goals which are formulated by its leaders, and to keep the society so mobile that nonparty groups have little chance to stabilize and thus exercise effective influence on its character. Thus, what is often called "permanent revolution" characterizes these regimes. The early Soviet Five-Year Plans were major instruments of social and economic revolution backed by fear, force, and measurable, though often unattainable, production goals. Moreover, in the background of all totalitarian regimes—and sometimes in the foreground—is the purge: a technique of government with its own positive as well as negative features.

THE PURGE

The purge promotes specific policies at the same time that it removes those who oppose them. It may eliminate, displace, or undercut the power of those against whom it is aimed. It acts against those considered a danger to the ruling elite either because they hold different social objectives (as was true of sizable groups in the early days of fascist and of Communist regimes) or because they endorse different techniques for moving toward the common goal (as did those in the Soviet Union who in the 1920's and again in early post-Stalinist days emphasized the need for consumers' goods rather than the concentration on heavy industry) or because they threaten to establish the predominant influence of a nonparty group (as in Hitler's purges of the military, and, notably in the case of Khrushchev, the managers of state-owned industry, the so-called economic bureaucracy, whose influence over production and distribution in their own segments of the economy was skillfully replaced from June, 1957, on by party control).

NAZI TOTALITARIANISM

It may perhaps be questioned whether the Nazi system, though totalitarian in its use of the purge and in its total interference—in theory as well as practice—with all spheres of life and society, also shared the other characteristic of Communist totalitarian regimes: their social and economic dynamism. Initially, the Hitler regime did not affect such established institutions as business enterprises and private property; through steadily increasing control of economic as well as all other matters, it tended more and more, however, to deprive such institutions of their usual functions. Of what use were private holdings, in practice, when all discretion of the holder to plan production, employ labor, and determine wage and price policies was taken away through over-all control by planning agencies, which, in turn, were dependent on the varying policies of the political leadership? And, particularly, of what use were they when the holder, like any other individual, might at any time disappear in a concentration camp in case he failed to comply? Hitler himself once commented that there was no need to socialize the means through which business and commerce were carried on, since "we socialize human beings." In addition, Nazism showed signs in its later stages of carrying through a more radical transformation of the economic and social structure, and it may be doubted whether capitalism—or any other traditional system or structure—could have endured if the Nazi system itself had lasted.

DEVELOPING STATES BETWEEN DEMOCRACY AND TOTALITARIANISM

Rapid social and economic change is the objective not only of totalitarian states, but also of many of the new, developing countries of Asia, Africa, and the Middle East which are striving to achieve modernity in record time. Their leaders face an obvious temptation to adopt totalitarian techniques to achieve this difficult purpose. Yet the appeals of totalitarianism are counterbalanced by its price. Totalitarianism demands a radical reorganization of society, which has its heaviest impact on the landed peasantry, the base of all underdeveloped countries. It tends to make the power structure rigid at a time when new national leaders seek to give their people a feeling of participation in the exercise of authority and thereby to legitimize their claims to supersede traditional authorities. It limits their opportunities to secure aid from the West as well as the East when most of them prefer to remain uncommitted to either.

For these reasons, the leaders of developing countries often attempt to combine features of both democratic and totalitarian systems. They organize state-directed community action at the same time that they foster individual enterprise. They favor one-party regimes without, however, crushing opportunities for individual or group opposition to particular programs or techniques. They sometimes incorporate the opposition, as in Guinea, rather than eliminate it by force. They attempt to secure majority or even universal support by the popularity of their efforts to promote national growth and international recognition. As in India, they maintain the flexibility and experimental approach which are characteristically democratic at the same time that they race ahead with far-reaching economic projects.

No one can say with assurance whether the developing states will be able to establish the framework of stability within which flexible change most fruitfully takes place; whether they can establish the norms of action which underpin the authority of administrators; and whether they can transform traditional societies through persuasion rather than compulsion. Many people deny that democracy is suitable, or even feasible, for societies with low levels of literacy, minimal standards of living for the bulk of their people, and few resources. These comments can be better evaluated after the more careful study of systems of government and the workings of institutions to which much of this book is devoted. It is worth noting here however, that the leaders of many of the developing states believe their states are and will remain democratic, and are working for this objective.

IS DEMOCRACY ADEQUATE FOR MODERN CONDITIONS?

While some people believe that only mature countries like Great Britain, the United States, Canada, and Sweden can maintain democracy under current conditions of international strain and the competition of totalitarian states, others question whether democracy is a workable system even for the Anglo-Saxon and European states which have been most successful in practicing it in the past. They maintain that its machinery is inadequate to modern needs. They assert that democracy's assumptions about tolerance, discussion, responsible leadership, and willingness to experiment are based on an unrealistic expectation of rationality and maturity on the part of ordinary individuals and, more particularly, of their leaders. And they affirm further that the totalitarian ideology has a more compelling attraction than has democracy in the relatively rootless, industrialized, and urbanized society of today. These criticisms of, and doubts about, democracy thus fall into three categories: the adequacy of its machinery; the assumptions it makes about human capacities; and the strength of its appeal in an age of uncertainty and tension. In addition, these same people query democracy's capacity to deal effectively with foreign affairs in the nuclear age, a problem which will be taken up later on.

IS ITS MACHINERY SUITABLE?

As to the machinery of democracy, it is questioned whether executives can be decisive and far-sighted at the same time that they are responsible to the public. Moreover, can democratic leaders afford to be influenced by what are perhaps passing currents of opinion, it is asked, when the issues they deal with affect such all-important questions as national security? In addition, can the public be trusted to select for the chief offices of state persons who possess judgment and capacities of leadership? In other words, is there not a basic inconsistency in the notion that efficiency can be combined with responsibleness? If it is said in answer that elected leaders provide the responsible element in a democracy, while professional administrators carry out the technical tasks of government, the comment may well be made that this association of elected amateurs with permanent professionals may mean in practice that the latter make the decisions and the former only provide a façade.

Further questions are raised by the critics of democracy about the adequacy of representative institutions to provide a link between the public and the possessors of political power. Is the right to cast a ballot once every year, or every five years, a meaningful form of political participation, they ask? Even those who work hard within a party organization may find themselves without influence on policy, it is said, since parties are run from behind the scenes by cliques or "bosses" for their own interests. Moreover, it is charged that pressure groups, far from broadening the concern of public figures with community interests, merely focus attention on particular and frequently only local demands, to the detriment of the public at large. Under such circumstances, legislatures are said to be mere conglomerations of warring interests, each seeking to secure the largest slice of public monies for itself. This becomes the easier, it is pointed out, because most representatives come from constituencies which have little sense of cohesion and, therefore, rarely attempt to influence the votes which are being cast in their name. In any case, it is sometimes questioned whether one man can ever represent the interests and thinking of another, and whether, therefore, the whole notion of representative government is not based on a false premise. To this is added the charge that the information on which the citizen depends both for his judgments on public policy and for making his choice of representatives is apt to be distorted to their own interests by those who control the media of communication: the press, radio, and TV.

ARE ITS ASSUMPTIONS TENABLE?

The next level of doubts about democracy concerns the capacity of ordinary human beings to make judgments on the complex issues of a modern state. On the one hand, it is pointed out that more and more of the responsibilities of government are technical in character, whether they are concerned with giant roads and bridges or with nuclear power. Moreover, many of the issues which must be decided affect the allocation of resources. But, in addition to questioning the adequacy of average people to make decisions on the affairs and personnel of a government concerned with such matters, there is the nagging uncertainty about whether people can retain that sense of detachment which permits them to separate public needs from their own private and selfish interests, whether they can listen judiciously to both sides of an argument, and whether they will refrain from violence when unpopular programs are put into effect.

HOW STRONG IS ITS APPEAL?

Finally, in what may well be the deepest of all challenges, it is questioned whether democracy, with its lack of assured program and goals, can answer with anything like the same success as can ideological totalitarianism the need of people for a faith.

This is an age when transcendental religion has lost its hold on many people, and yet it is one in which strains and uncertainties create a particular need for spiritual reinforcement. Fascist or Communist ideologies, with their popular symbols and their certainty about their goals, offer the appeal of a new religion to many who are living in a spiritual vacuum. Even if democracy may be said to satisfy its mature practitioners, there are many who doubt that it can equal the attraction of a totalitarian faith either to those within Western countries who find themselves disadvantaged in the competition for the good things of life, or, more especially, to the still underdeveloped, oftentimes hungry and suffering majority of the world's people, whether in Asia, Africa, or Latin America.

Such an indictment of democracy as has been made brings to the surface some of the commonplaces of political comment; it does little to test their validity. It provides a background, however, against which much of the rest of this book can examine the workings of institutions of mature democracies as well as of developing states and of modern fascist and Communist dictatorships. Politics has the right to be ranked as a science only in so far as its processes are analyzed with the same care as is given to the data of what are commonly called the experimental sciences. This work makes no pretensions to developing a new theory of politics, but it does attempt to examine the workings of different types of political systems and to evaluate their consequences in the light of such information as we now possess. If in so doing it stimulates discussion on the validity of the questions and on the doubts about democracy which have been raised, and on ways in which these questions and doubts might be answered, this, too, will fit into the purpose of the book.

III

PATTERNS OF GOVERNMENT

Despite the vast variety of political forms which exist throughout the world, there are certain particularly significant patterns of government which have emerged, partly out of history, partly out of force, and partly out of example. These chief patterns of government are those of the *one-party dictatorship,* whether Communist or fascist; the *parliamentary* pattern of Great Britain and the Commonwealth and the somewhat different parliamentary patterns of Western and Northern European countries; and the *presidential* pattern of the United States. To a large extent, these three systems have been adopted by—or imposed upon—most of the countries of the world, and it is particularly important, therefore, to understand their basic features.

THE ONE-PARTY DICTATORSHIP

The simplest of all modern political forms is the one-party dictatorship. Its concentration of political authority in the hands of the executive and administration is underpinned by the all-pervasive influence of a highly organized political party which can scarcely be differentiated from the governmental machinery which it operates. Though representative organs are commonly a part of the structure of modern one-party dictatorships, it is not their purpose to provide control, but rather to serve as a sounding board for political pronouncements. Law and the courts do not operate as separate independent entities authorized to decide disputes concerning the operations of other governmental organs, but act to reinforce the norms of behavior laid down by the party leadership and ratified by the executive and administration. This remains true even when these norms are radically changed in response to new objectives. Thus, it is characteristic of one-party dictatorships that all the organs of government—executive, administrative, legislative, and judicial—find their overriding purpose in the objectives of the regime, and that these objectives are formulated by the leaders of the one political party which infiltrates and directs not only political, but also economic, social, and, in principle, even highly personal affairs.

Having said this, however, it is necessary to point out that within this over-all definition of the one-party dictatorship, there is a wide variety in the ways in which its instrumentalities are used and the purposes to which they are directed. Fascist states, like Hitler's Germany and, though somewhat less so, Mussolini's Italy, were molded by particular appeals (Hitler to "blood and soil," Mussolini to the glories of ancient Rome) which tended to make them *sui generis,* while Communism has certain universal tenets and notions of historical evolution which provide a compulsion toward unity and uniformity among Communist states. However, despite this compulsion toward a general unity, there is increasing evidence of variety among the Communist states themselves, with Poland, for example, tending to modify dictatorial practices and slowing down the processes of social and economic change, while China presses ahead the socialization of agriculture and village life and the "communization" of all life with a rapidity and ruthlessness greater even than that used in the early days of the Five-Year Plans of the Soviet Union. Within the Soviet Union itself, which has had by far the longest history of any of the modern one-party dictatorships, it is now possible to identify three eras: the revolutionary mass-party movement of Lenin, organized and carried through under disciplined leadership, but still retaining its appeal for popular support; the strongly statist regime of Stalin, in which centralized authority backed by brutality and frequent purges forced a social and economic revolution in order to create a powerful industrial structure; and the Khrushchev era, with its greater flexibility combined with increased party control operating through local as well as central organs.

Nonetheless, despite great differences in their use of power and even in the allocation of authority, there is relatively little variation among the one-party dictatorships in the political form itself. The key remains the concentration of power in a single party whose influence permeates every aspect of life and which provides the most powerful means of centralized and all-pervasive rule which has yet been developed.

THE PARLIAMENTARY PATTERN

The pattern of dictatorship is a relatively simple one; the forms of democratic states have endless variety. They revolve around various methods of attempting to secure those purposes of which we spoke when discussing democracy: an effective representation of the electorate; a relation between the organs of representation and the executive which permits leadership and, at the same time, keeps it in constant touch with the elected representatives of the people; and limits on arbitrary use of power by government and its officials. The methods adopted by particular states arise out of historical evolution (particularly obvious in relation to Great Britain); or out of concepts modified by evolution (as in the United States); or out of attempts to correct past inadequacies (as in the Fifth French Republic, with its great strengthening of the executive to avoid the legislative omnipotence and executive instability of the Fourth and even Third French Republics, or as in West Germany); or out of transfer of institutions to former dependent territories (as in the Commonwealth of Nations); or out of a combination of these factors. Within the wide range of democratic forms of government, the most common is the parliamentary pattern, partly because of the influence of British parliamentary experience, but more particularly because of its relative simplicity of organization and apparent ease of operation.

The prime characteristic of the parliamentary form of government is the so-called fusion of the executive and legislature. The executive becomes the governing group not because of a direct vote by the electorate, as in the presidential system, but because it comprises the leaders of one or several parties represented in the legislature who are able to command sufficient support within that body to pass the legislation embodied in their program. In a two-party system, there is no question about which party commands a majority in the legislature; its leaders assume the executive role as soon as an election has made this clear. In a multiparty system, there may well be more difficulty about determining which combination of leaders shall assume the role of the executive. In either case, however, there is an interaction between executive and legislature which keeps them constantly interrelated and dependent on each other but, at the same time, fulfilling different functions. The executive organizes the program, pushes it through the legislature by personal and direct leadership, and supervises the administration. The members of the legislature consider the details of the program, criticize or support the executive's and the administration's handling of their responsibilities, and keep alert to the comments of their constituents and to the general reactions of the country to governmental policy. Within the parliamentary system, therefore, there is an intimate association of the executive and legislature, combined with differentiation of function; there is effective government (at least where the parliamentary majority is clear), combined with opportunities—as through the daily question period in the British parliamentary system—for making the executive justify its actions.

Technically, the parliamentary system revolves around the institution of (and procedures of expressing or denying) "confidence" in the executive. Where parliament can force the government (in the sense of the executive) to resign by voting "nonconfidence" in it—or at least compel the executive to dissolve parliament in such a case and appeal to the electorate—the parliamentary system is operating in its classic form. Systems, such as those of present-day France and West Germany, which render such expression of confidence or nonconfidence difficult, if not impossible, are thus of doubtful parliamentary nature; rather, as we suggested earlier, they are on the verge of authoritarianism (though one which is limited in time due to legally required periodic elections).

The close working together of executive and legislature within the framework of the parliamentary system contrasts with the nonpolitical nature of the judiciary. Judicial independence, which is essential for the maintenance of limitations on political and administrative actions, must be a principle of government in a democratic state; it is reinforced by the fact that judges are chosen from a particular profession (in Great Britain from senior barristers, i.e., those who plead cases in the law courts; in the United States also from the legal profession; and in France and Germany from persons trained for this particular career) and that they have permanence of tenure. In Great Britain and France, courts of law do not pass on the constitutionality of legislative acts, but in some parliamentary systems, like those of Canada, Australia, West Germany, and Austria, cases can be taken to a supreme court to determine the constitutionality of legislation in the light of the basic constitutional document. In all democratic systems, however, one court or another can make judgments on the legality of administrative acts by testing them against the statute or ordinance under which the action was taken.

THE BRITISH PARLIAMENTARY SYSTEM

The British parliamentary system, often looked on as a model of effective yet responsible government, evolved out of two counterprocesses which operated at different periods of time. The first process was one of differentiation of functions which had originally emanated from the person of the monarch, and subsequently one of limitations on his power. This long process led to the separate jurisdiction of the courts of law, and to documents—notably

Magna Carta in 1215, the Petition of Right in 1628, and the Bill of Right in 1689—which attempted to prevent the monarch from acting in what was looked on as an arbitrary fashion destructive of customary rights. In the seventeenth century, the House of Commons with its twofold influence—as a grantor of money and as a representative body—assumed the leading role in attempting to limit the monarch, while the execution of Charles I and the deposition of James II made it quite clear that royal power could never again be supreme. The second process began in the mid-eighteenth century, when the king commenced to select his chief advisers or ministers from persons who had the confidence and support of a majority of the members in the House of Commons. As this principle became established, the reasons for limiting the powers of the Crown disappeared. Thus the British Cabinet, which now wields the powers of the Crown, possesses a wide measure of independent executive authority as well as the power it secures through its leadership of the legislative body.

This leadership, in contrast to what we may call the "French" type of parliamentarism (i.e., of the Third and Fourth French Republics), issues not only from the traditional British two-party system, which ordinarily guarantees majority party control in the House of Commons, but also from the established right of the Crown (now exercised by the Prime Minister) to dissolve Parliament. The nonexistence or nonexercise of such a right in the "French" system, on the other hand, accounted for the weakness of the executive and the predominance of Parliament in the structure of the latter system.

Though the British Cabinet is one of the most powerful executive bodies in the democratic world because of its control of the House of Commons, it nevertheless accepts its responsibility to act for the country as a whole and not merely as the organ of the majority party. It is kept on the *qui vive* by the constant probing and questioning of the opposition party and by the publicity given to governmental actions and policies by the more responsible portions of the press, and by radio and TV. In a somewhat similar combination of freedom for and restraint on governmental action, the courts in Great Britain do not question the validity of an act of Parliament, but in handling a case in which it is relevant they proceed from the premise that legislation is meant to be reasonable in intent, that is, to deal fairly and equally with all people. Coupled with the bias toward individual freedom of the common law, out of which have come many of the basic rules of procedure and precedents which mold the workings and judgments of the courts, this "rule of reason" reinforces the civil liberties of which the British are justly proud.

THE PARLIAMENTARY SYSTEM IN THE COMMONWEALTH

The British parliamentary system evolved out of history and through a process extending over centuries. All the more remarkable, therefore, has been the extension of British parliamentary institutions into the countries of the British Empire and thus into the Commonwealth of Nations. Rarely have institutions resembled so closely the parent stock as those of Canada, Australia, New Zealand, and (to a certain extent) South Africa. In each of these, there can be found the system of cabinet responsibility, the parliamentary concentration of power, and what is in essence the two-party system so characteristic of Great Britain.

Yet history and environment have added individual

features of major importance in each of these countries. Thus, Canada and Australia are federal systems in which the territorial division of power strains constantly against the unifying pressures of parliamentary rule; moreover, judicial review has played a far greater role in their development than it could in the unitary states of Great Britain and New Zealand and the quasi-unitary state of South Africa in which the territorial division of functions has no constitutional guarantee. As far as party systems are concerned, Canada follows the American pattern more than it does the British, with both its major parties, the Liberals and Conservatives, functioning as great holding companies of diverse interests and only the minority CCF (Cooperative Commonwealth Federation) unified by a social program comparable to that of the Labour Parties of Great Britain, Australia, and New Zealand. When we look at policies, we find that Australia and New Zealand took the lead in early and radical experiments with state ownership and with compulsory arbitration of industrial disputes.

But whatever their divergence from British forms, Canada, Australia, and New Zealand (though not South Africa under its Afrikaner Nationalist Government) have a basic similarity to Great Britain in political tradition and constitutional attitudes which is far more significant. Underlying this similarity there is not only a common intellectual and political heritage—kept strong by ties of blood constantly refreshed by immigration and by allegiance to a common Crown—but there are also the virtually ideal conditions for democracy possessed by these overseas parts of the Commonwealth. Notable among these conditions are their middle-class structures (so important, as Aristotle pointed out long ago, for the harmonious working of a constitution), widespread economic prosperity, a high degree of social mobility, and a workable balance between industry and agriculture. None of these criteria holds true, of course, for South Africa's numerically predominant non-white population; and though some are valid for its white minority, which still holds the monopoly of political and economic power and social prestige, it has not exhibited, especially in the last decade, the same scrupulousness for constitutional forms as do the other three countries.

Far more remarkable than finding British institutions and parliamentary traditions operating in the older parts of the Commonwealth overseas is to find them also in several of the newer Commonwealth members: India, Malaya, and Nigeria. Here the rate of literacy is low, the middle class is a small if dominant minority, and poverty is widespread. Yet despite such handicaps, these countries have had considerable success so far in holding democratic elections (using symbols on the ballots, since the overwhelming proportion of voters cannot read), in operating parliamentary institutions, and even in handling that part of government most difficult for the inexperienced—administration.

This experience is reassuring, in view of the considerable number of non-Western or only partially Western states which may soon be acquiring independence and membership in the Commonwealth: the West Indian Federation and the Federation of Rhodesia and Nyasaland (if they can hold their units together), Sierra Leone, and, possibly, the predominantly African but somewhat multiracial East African territories—Kenya, Uganda, and Tanganyika. All of these states have one thing in common: their experience under British tutelage with British-type institutions and traditions. These emerging states, however, (with the exception of Southern Rhodesia) have had far less practice in administration than India; moreover, none of them has yet acquired, to any considerable degree, that overriding loyalty to the interest of the state as compared to that of clan, group, or family which insulates administration against corruption. Thus the degree to which, in practice, they can or will maintain the British pattern of government remains to be seen.

THE PARLIAMENTARY SYSTEM IN WESTERN EUROPE

But the British pattern is only one facet of what is still the most widespread form of democratic political organization today: the parliamentary system. Though in general that system is characterized by the dependence of the executive on the confidence of the legislature, there can be wide differences in executive-legislative relations. In the British form of parliamentary government, the executive dominates the legislature, partly because, with rare exceptions, it is not parliament, but the people through their votes who, in practice, choose the executive. In a sense, therefore, the legislature in British countries acts like an electoral college, as far as the creation of ministries is concerned, though, unlike other electoral colleges, it continues in existence, discussing, criticizing, and passing upon the policies of the ministry. In the traditional French system, on the other hand, the legislature dominated the ministry because it had created the ministry. A net result of these and other differences is that while Great Britain has a strong, stable Cabinet, France used to have a weak, unstable one.

France

What we have called the traditional French system is that of the Third Republic and of the Fourth Republic (which came into being at the end of World War II and ended in 1958). The Third, and even more the Fourth Republic provide obvious examples of the problems which arise when a too-powerful legislature, torn by a multiparty system (in which, after World War II, both the extreme left—the Communists—and the extreme right—for a time the Poujadists—were antidemocratic), results in an unstable executive incapable of providing consistent and effective leadership. The Constitution of the Fifth French Republic is designed to correct this imbalance and has done so to such a degree that France, since 1958, has been governed by what is less a parliamentary regime than a mixture of authoritarianism and technocracy, with technical experts directing administration under the general supervision of the Cabinet (of which they are important members) and of the President, General Charles de Gaulle.

Under the Fifth French Republic, no Cabinet member may also be a member of the National Assembly, as all members were in the Fourth French Republic, though he can appear before that body to direct discussions and explain policy. The Cabinet in the new regime has specified independent powers it did not possess before, while the Assembly, far from being omnipotent, appears almost impotent, being limited in its periods of meeting and restricted in debate. The President is no longer selected by the votes of the National Assembly and Senate meeting jointly, as under the Fourth French Republic (on one occasion, the crippling force of party divisions necessitated more than one hundred ballots), but by elected local office holders throughout the country. In the person of De Gaulle, the President not only possesses substantial reserve powers under which he can act if the Cabinet ceases to provide effective executive control, but also vast personal prestige which gives the regime something of the character of a monarchy of the days when the king ruled as well as reigned.

West Germany

It may be asked whether the Gaullist system of the Fifth Republic fits into a kind of prototype of regimes in-between traditional parliamentarism and new-style authoritarianism. Seeing what has emerged in West Germany since World War II, it is difficult to deny a trend toward such a form. In West Germany, one of the remarkable group of "grand old men" currently or recently determining the fates of nations has had a dominating influence in providing effective leadership within what had been conceived of as basically a parliamentary type of government. To be sure, to compare Chancellor Konrad Adenauer's "democratur" (a kind of dictatorial democracy, as his rule has sometimes, and perhaps not quite fairly, been referred to) with the at least half-authoritarian structure of the French Fifth Republic is not entirely appropriate. But there are features of the Bonn system which warrant some doubt as to whether a genuine parliamentary democracy is emerging, or surviving, in West Germany.

It is clear that the system was intended to provide Germans with a genuine parliamentary pattern of government. But the pre-Nazi Weimar system, whose extreme parliamentarianism had resulted in an instability comparable to that of the Third French Republic, had a strong influence on the drafters of the Bonn Constitution. Consequently, they devised built-in guarantees of executive stability, such as the so-called "constructive vote of nonconfidence," which makes it necessary for a party or parties desiring to overthrow the incumbent Chancellor to present a candidate backed by a new majority before the incumbent can be forced to resign.

Since in other respects the Federal Assembly constitutionally enjoys the customary rights and privileges of a parliament in a full-fledged parliamentary democracy, this stipulation might not have been so decisive, however, had not other factors combined to strengthen the executive at the expense of the powers and prestige of parliament. Under any circumstances, a country like Germany, unused in the past to the ways and habits of government by discussion and consent, would have had a hard time growing into such ways of political life. As it happened, the forceful personality of Adenauer, the very prototype of the German expert-politician interested in *having things done* rather than in *how* they are done, presided over the reconstruction of West Germany after the Nazi breakdown and defeat. By good luck and management, this reconstruction period proved to be one of unexcelled economic prosperity as well as unequalled rise to eminence in the foreign field, thereby greatly contributing to the reputation of his government. To Germans, habitually looking to the expert leader in political, executive, and administrative affairs to handle matters without much participation and initiative on their part, Adenauer's regime provided a chance to see efficiency combined with representative government. But the latter was bound to suffer. Adenauer lost no time in establishing the principle that ministers, far from being coresponsible members of the Cabinet and separately responsible to Parliament, are his own aides exclusively. In addition, many fields, such as foreign affairs, have for all practical purposes been eliminated from parliamentary purview, and the prestige and standing of the *Bundestag* has therefore steadily declined in the public eye.

One more trend has contributed to this process, the trend toward what is less a two-party system than a "one-and-a-half party" system. Since the Christian Democrats have been in office under Adenauer's leadership since the inception of the Bonn regime, the other major party, the Social Democrats, have been left in ineffectual and frustrated opposition, an opposition which has found little outlet through debate and criticism in Parliament or elsewhere. In neither economic nor foreign affairs have they found policy alternatives which can be fused into an attractive program. Thus, the Social Democrats are unlikely to be able to make those inroads into the nonlabor part of the electorate which would give them a genuine chance to become the majority party. There is a chance, therefore, of perpetuating the control of the present governing party under its dominant leader. As in France, of course, the question arises as to what will happen to such a system once the chief figure—De Gaulle or Adenauer—disappears. Germany, perhaps even more than France, may find it difficult to operate a stable parliamentary democracy, for which as yet the roots have not sunk far.

Italy

There remains only one major country in continental Europe—Italy—where the traditional parliamentary system still holds sway. The numerous falls and crises of government which it has suffered since the end of the war remind one of the Third and Fourth French Republics rather than of Great Britain. Moreover, the future of the parliamentary system seems particularly endangered in Italy because of the radicalism of the party, or, counting the Nenni Socialists separately, the parties in permanent opposition, and the dependence of the ruling Christian Democrats on the uncertain backing of one or more small groups.

On the other hand, as we survey other Western European parliamentary systems, we find that most of them work better and are more stable.

The Netherlands and Scandinavia

In the Netherlands, Norway, Sweden, and Switzerland, the executive is weaker than in Great Britain, but much more stable than in France's Fourth Republic. In the Netherlands, for example, the multiparty system throws the choice of the ministry into the chamber; there are occasional cabinet crises lasting several months before a ministry is formed. But once selected, the Cabinet and even more the Prime Minister tend to retain office for relatively long periods of time. This can partly be explained by two characteristics of these parliamentary systems: the fact that Cabinet and legislature are more separated from each other than in Britain or West Germany, and yet that there is a great deal more give-and-take between the two in hammering out the legislative program.

These Western European countries thus have a very different view than do the British of what should be the relation between the executive and the legislature. The executive in the Scandinavian countries and in the Netherlands tends both to bargain more and to be more adjustable. To have the legislature reject an important part of the cabinet's program is not looked on as a major defeat, as it would be in Britain. On the contrary, when the executive brings forward a project, it anticipates not only that this project will be carefully considered in the legislature, as is true in Great Britain, but possibly also modified, and it accepts this situation. Thus, these countries tread a middle way between the possible "cabinet dictatorship" of the British parliamentary system (which, in Britain itself, is avoided by the self-restraint of the Cabinet, but which has occurred in South Africa, when the Nationalist Government used a slim majority to force through controversial legislation) and the executive instability of the Fourth French Republic. The result is a system marked by compromise and a genuine executive-legislative partnership in the making of law.

Switzerland

The relation between parliament and executive in Switzerland deviates from the usual parliamentary pattern to such an extent that some students of comparative government consider the "Swiss system" to be a third type, to be distinguished from either the normal parliamentary or the presidential system. Once elected by parliament, the federal councilors who make up the seven-member Swiss executive never resign over any issue of policy which divides them, individually or as a body, from a parliamentary majority. They continue to preside over their departments, following the instructions of Parliament. Since, furthermore, Parliament cannot be dissolved under the Swiss system, the political interplay between legislature and executive which is characteristic of other parliamentary systems, and which may lead to resignations, dissolutions, and new elections in the wake of votes of nonconfidence, does not exist in Switzerland. This shows that the Swiss executive is a top-level bureaucracy rather than a policy-making, issue-resolving separate "power." Issues are resolved either in parliament or by popular vote (initiative and referendum), a characteristic Swiss institution. Since Switzerland's permanent neutrality prejudges most of its foreign-policy problems, issues tend, however, to be less serious and numerous than in other Western European democracies.

The bureaucratic nature of the Swiss executive is further apparent from the customarily long tenure of individual councilors, extending frequently over many parliamentary terms. These re-elections are possible because—in another deviation from the usual parliamentary pattern—the Federal Council comprises representatives of all the major parties regardless of election results, although not on a proportionate basis. Moreover, the body functions as a truly collegiate group. There is nobody who might be compared to a prime minister, not even as "first among equals." This reflects the fact that the Swiss executive does not provide political leadership. In a way, Switzerland has perhaps the truest "parliamentary" system of all, since Parliament is in charge of all important decisions and the executive is a mere committee of that body, without political ambitions of its own. There, the system has been highly successful in combining democratic responsibility and representation with stability of government. But it is questionable whether it could function equally well in larger and more divided nations which lack the broad constitutional and general consensus with which the closely knit Swiss community is blessed.

Austria

A still different and even stranger kind of system has developed in postwar Austria. There, in striking contrast to Switzerland, Parliament has been emasculated both in its role as legislature and as supervisor of the executive by virtue of the fact that the two major parties, the Socialists and the People's Party (which in postwar elections have always been almost equal in strength) work together in a government coalition which leaves little room for effective opposition. The resulting executive "cartel" functions on the basis of an initial compact which, clearly and in detail, outlines those policies which are agreed upon and, in consequence, are not opposed by either of the two parties in the Cabinet or Parliament. The machinery of administration, in turn, is divided among the two parties on the basis of "parity," so that for each position which is assigned to one there is an equivalent office for the other. Jokingly it has been asked whether, in case one tenor at the Vienna State Opera happens to be from the People's Party, there must be another with Socialist affiliation. This division of state offices and the absence of effective opposition have their obvious shortcomings; but the system is defended by Austrians as a far lesser evil than the possible alternative, which existed in the post-World War I period, in which social classes and their party representatives were so deeply divided that they ultimately clashed in a civil war in 1934. While the earlier Austrian experience terminated in dictatorship, the present one at least permits the functioning of a system, pseudoparliamentary though it may be, that seems to guarantee the peaceful coexistence of the two parties without major infractions of individual or group rights and liberties.

What is apparent from such a survey is that the parliamentary system is infinitely flexible in adapting to local situations and traditions. By facilitating close executive-legislative relations, this system makes it easy to combine leadership with representative institutions. Familiarity with the parliamentary form may have been an important reason why former colonies of Great Britain, France, and the Netherlands have adopted it on achieving their independence, but it is also attractive because of its easy adaptability to their particular needs. In practice, almost all of the newer nations have established parliamentary institutions rather than the presidential system which, in an earlier generation, was adopted by the newly independent states of Latin America and by Liberia.

The Presidential Pattern

The presidential pattern of government is the other great type of representative democracy. Its distinctive feature, in contrast to parliamentary government, is that the chief executive holds office whether or not he is supported by the majority of members of the legislature. As the 1956 American election demonstrated, the voters may even elect a Republican President at the same moment that they provide a Democratic majority in both the House of Representatives and the Senate. Under these circumstances, there is an extreme example of the constant give-and-take between executive and legislature that characterizes Continental parliamentary systems like those of Norway and the Netherlands. Even when the American President's party dominates the legislature, the President has less assured control over the passage of laws than even a weak British Prime Minister. Yet at the same time, there are great resources at the disposal of an American President. He is leader of his party, he controls the administration, and he can appeal directly to the people to support his program. Underwriting these sources of power is his guaranteed possession of office for four years, twice the life of the lower house.

As with the British parliamentary system, the characteristic features of the American presidential system are founded in history. It is important to remember that the American Constitution was drafted not in 1776, at the moment of proclaiming independence from Great Britain, when reaction against executive power was at its height, but in 1787, over a decade later, when the balance had swung sharply, and many of the framers of the Constitution thought dangerously, in favor of powerful legislatures within the states which were enacting radical economic measures in response to the pressures of popular majorities. The Constitution was thus designed to erect a strong national government which could curb the excesses of the states in the interests of financial stability, and within that national government to establish effective checks on the power of the lower house, the most direct agent of the people.

Hence it provided for the establishment of a strong second chamber, the Senate, whose members were originally appointed by state legislatures and for six year terms, in contrast to the two-year terms of representatives in the lower house. Hence, too, it safeguarded the independence of the chief executive, the President, whose selection through an electoral college was intended to make him only indirectly responsible to the people, and whose four-year term completes the pattern of staggered elections. The President was given the power to veto laws, to nominate officials, and to command the army. Moreover, although his veto of laws can be overriden by a two-thirds majority of the members of both the Senate and the House of Representatives, the Constitution provided for the so-called "pocket veto," which makes it impossible to override a presidential veto of measures passed at the end of a congressional session.

Lastly, to complete the pattern of checks and balances within the national government, there is the strong position of the federal judiciary (whose members are appointed for life by the President with the consent of the Senate) and, in particular, of the Supreme Court. Whether the framers of the Constitution intended the Supreme Court to have the power of judicial review is still disputed, but in practice it has exercised that power since Chief Justice John Marshall claimed it in Marbury vs. Madison in 1803. His decision, in 1819, in McCulloch vs. Maryland opened the way to a continuous broadening of the powers and functions of the national government by asserting that the Constitution provides implied as well as explicitly delegated powers. This means that Congress may choose whatever means it considers appropriate for carrying out its legitimate purposes, as long as these means are not specifically prohibited. No less significant, the judgment reaffirmed the precedent that it is the Supreme Court which determines whether or not an act of Congress is constitutional, i.e., has binding force because it is enacted out of legally possessed powers.

Not only is the American presidential system characterized by the *functional* division of national power, maintained by the checks and balances between the three, specifically separated, branches—the executive, legislature and judiciary—but also by the *territorial* division of power between the federal government and those of the states. It would have been impossible to establish a national government in 1787 without leaving a considerable amount of power in the hands of the state units which had been exercising independent authority since the Declaration of Independence. Federalism was also looked on as a further application of the theory of checks and balances by which rash acts on the part of individual states could be restrained.

Some of the obviously restrictive features of the original Constitution have been changed by formal amendment. Since 1913, Senators have been elected directly by the voters of their states; the franchise has been broadened, and constitutional provisions forbid discrimination on grounds of sex or race (though Americans still face serious problems in preventing the latter). But by far the greatest changes have come through what may be called the unwritten constitution which has grown up alongside the formal Constitution. Party activities, nominating conventions, the President's Cabinet, all these are part of the unwritten constitution which has arisen out of usage, judicial decisions, and legislation. The popular control which keeps both executive and legislature in the national and state spheres responsive to public pressure is almost entirely the result of an evolution which has gone on both inside and outside the formal Constitution.

Despite this evolution, and its basic responsiveness to popular sentiment, the American presidential system remains characterized by built-in restraints and the balance of powers. While the machinery of government can act swiftly in response to a national need such as posed by war or depression, the constitutional provisions for dividing authority—separation of powers, bicameralism (of two more or less equally powerful chambers), and judicial review—combine to prevent or impede major changes in policy until public pressures have built up on a broad scale. Whereas the parliamentary system responds quickly to popular majorities, the American presidential system reinforces the position of powerful and organized minorities, e.g., of Middle Western farm interests and of white

Patterns of Government

Southerners through their disproportionately high representation (in proportion to population) in the Senate and on committees of the House of Representatives and Senate concerned with issues in which they have particular interest.

It is at the committee level that the power structure within Congress has so much effect. In contrast to the Cabinet's constant control of legislation and of the budget in the British parliamentary system, specialized committees of Congress determine the fate not only of legislation proposed by their own members, but also of proposals for legislative and budgetary measures which come from the chief executive. Woodrow Wilson once characterized the American system as "a government by the chairmen of the standing committees of Congress." Under the seniority rule, committee chairmen become such because they have been on a committee longer than any other member of the party holding a majority in that chamber. This provides a strong advantage to those states or districts which re-elect their representatives over and over again: among the Republicans, this advantage accrues to some of the Northern areas; among the Democrats, to the South. Since party cohesion and discipline is far less strong in Congress than in the great majority of parliamentary systems, these provisions (which are based on convention and are not necessarily a part of the congressional-presidential system) reinforce the power position of certain local interests.

The person who believes strongly in majority rule and looks for a system which will smoothly and swiftly translate majority wishes into legislation will favor the parliamentary system over the presidential. The person who is concerned about the dangers of impulsive popular pressures and about the protection of vested groups and interests may well favor the presidential-congressional system. It is obvious that each has its own particular problems and requires a particular type of restraint and experience to operate in such a fashion as to secure effective results in needed legislation without degenerating into irresponsible majority rule.

Like the British parliamentary system of government, the American presidential system has provided a model for the government of many states. As noted above, the republics of Latin America have copied, to a greater or lesser extent, the structure devised by the American Constitution. Except in rare instances, this has been done of their own accord and not through any American tutelage comparable to the British and French experiments in developing colonies toward self-government through the progressive handing over of responsibility for operating their institutions. For better or, in some instances, for worse, Latin American countries and (though less so now) Liberia have had to struggle largely unaided to make their American-type institutions operate. In a considerable number of situations, as we will see, the results bear little resemblance to the parent model. This is sometimes true also in regard to those newer countries which have adopted the parliamentary system. Thus we may well ask: How deep does Western influence go among the developing countries of Latin America, Africa, the Middle East, and Asia?

HOW DEEP DOES WESTERN INFLUENCE GO?

Taking into account the degree of imitation of the governmental forms of Great Britain, France, the United States, and the Soviet Union, we might be tempted to say that the ideas of Locke and Harrington, Montesquieu and Rousseau, Bentham and Mill, and Hegel and Marx have been, by and large, the determinants of the modern world. But to what degree has this been more than a surface influence? Is it not possible that the century or more in which these ideas and their attendant institutions have flourished constitutes, at least for the non-Western world, what an Indian author recently called the "Vasco da Gama age"? In other words, has this perhaps been merely a transitory period of superficial Western influence over a non-Western world again shaping its own destinies? Or, to ask a different question: Has the Western influence in fact been strong enough to establish Western democratic ways in countries whose background and conditions of life are so essentially dissimilar to those of the middle-class democracies of the United States, Great Britain, Canada, Australia, and New Zealand?

If we study Latin-American life, for instance, we are struck by the frequent discrepancy between the constitutional framework (and its underlying ideological assumptions) and the political reality. The Latin-American mind —that is, the mind of its intellectuals—steeped as it is in Anglo-American or, more often, Continental-European traditions, tends to be legalistic; it loves to indulge in the niceties of formal constitutional arguments and interpretations without great regard as to whether they are meaningful. Actually, of course, one must distinguish between Latin-American states for which such a generalization is valid and those for which it is not. Advanced nations like Chile or Uruguay have been able to make institutions and constitutions of a Western type much more meaningful than others in South America, like Peru or Bolivia, where a majority of the population, in many cases Indians, still live under the primitive conditions of the age of discoveries; or where a one-crop or one-resource economy concentrates wealth in a tiny (formerly usually foreign, now mixed foreign-indigenous) upper class. In Chile and Uruguay, there exists a basis for political stability and even democracy. In the less advanced nations of Latin America, it is hardly surprising to find that political power tends to be concentrated in the hands of one man (the *caudillo*) or of a small group, commonly of military men (*junta*). Thus in the curious and extreme instance of the Dominican Republic, there has been a concentration of almost all the national wealth in the *caudillo's* own hands, for Trujillo, together with members of his family, owns most of the enterprises (which remain tax-exempt) and even a large part of the landed property of "his" country. In certain other instances, it is among a small number of educated and Europeanized families that political (together with economic and social) control has circulated.

Thus we see that constitutions and similar organizational rules can mean little; in some cases they may be merely convenient tools for attaining or maintaining power. In Honduras, for instance—to give an example of a situation which is not unique—the constitution provides that a president must stand for re-election after a certain period of office; if no candidate receives 51 per cent of the vote, congress is then empowered to elect the president by a two-thirds majority of the legal membership. But we soon discover that the incumbent usually knows how to get 51 per cent of the vote; if he has not received it, he may see to it that congress has no quorum, in which case the constitutional order is considered "broken" and the incumbent continues in power. Or, as often happens, a constitution which thus limits a president's term or his re-eligibility is simply "amended" (or replaced with a new one) so as to eliminate the obnoxious provision. Constitutions thus are liable to frequent and rapid change, often following upon a *Putsch*. Indeed, and paradoxically, it has even been said that something is wrong with political life in a Latin-American republic if there are no violent changes once in a while; for long-enduring quiet under one and the same constitution frequently indicates a protracted dictatorship, while a breach of the constitutional order may indicate democratic stirrings. More often, however, it merely indicates a change in top-level control.

The more advanced Latin-American countries rarely have this kind of *caudillo* regime. But even here, most of them enjoy neither the long tradition of liberal-democratic and constitutional ideas nor the broad middle class which promoted such ideas in the older democracies. As a consequence, their institutions are less stable than those of more mature democracies. Thus in a country like Brazil, democracy may alternate with dictatorship or, as happened in 1956, an army coup to forestall another antidemocratic coup may be required in order to enable the duly elected president to assume office. The progress to a stable constitutional order is thus frequently a halting one.

The importance of economic equality and lack of racial cleavage for the development of democratic constitutionalism is exemplified by the vivid contrast in Central America between democratic Costa Rica and its neighbors. The former has a broad and fairly equal distribution of land among an almost uniformly white population, whereas in the latter there are small, feudal elites of Spanish origin which own most of the wealth and control the predominant Indian or mixed population both economically and politically. The instability of these countries contrasts sharply with the continuity of democratic rule in Costa Rica. Still more striking, the efforts to restore constitutionalism after protracted periods of *caudillo* rule or civil war and to forestall new coups on the part of opposition parties has led Colombia to adopt a unique "system of alternation" in which, through solemn agreement between the two major groups, control is exercised first by the one and then by the other.

Paradoxically, the basis for liberal democratic developments is sometimes laid by a preliminary stage of what may be called an "educational dictatorship," which provides for the rapid modernization of a backward country. Turkey, in which Kemal Ataturk Westernized his nation by means of a dictatorship operating through a one-party system, provides an outstanding example. It is questionable, in fact, whether it would have been possible without his dictatorship to transform Turkey from a typically Oriental, Islamic, traditionalist country into a modern nation—considering that what was involved was not only drastic political and economic change, but the destruction of deeply rooted customs (the abolition of the harem, the veil, the fez, and the caliphate; and the introduction of the Western alphabet, script, and calendar, for example). As the Turkish experience seemed to show, gradual democratization may indeed follow such a transformation, though the re-establishment of army rule in 1960 would suggest that the foundation was less firmly established than had been hoped.

On the other hand, the old feudal interests or those of foreign capital may turn to their own purposes apparently democratic institutions, in particular parliaments which are controlled or have been bought by them. This was the situation in Egypt prior to its national revolution in 1953. It is still the case in Iran, where the feudal landowning interests dominate parliament, while the ruler himself, the Shah, has emerged as the leader of a movement to reshape the socioeconomic structure of the nation through agrarian reform. More often, however, the movement toward change comes from below and, in the name of economic and social reform (and often with an anti-Western or anti-"Yankee" slant), establishes a "Kemalist" type of regime, such as the Estenssoro rule in Bolivia, or the various Mexican regimes since that country's national revolution in 1917.

If economic, social, and cultural reforms lead toward eventual political democratization, then authoritarianism or even dictatorship may turn out to have been a blessing in disguise. But it is also true that the procedures used during the educational phase may of themselves create that corruption and cynicism which are so dangerous to genuine democracy. Thus, in the 1954 elections to the Iranian Majlis (parliament), bands of the Shah's supporters saw to it that his candidates won out over all others. As newspapers reported, "admiring police and soldiers frequently helped Shaban [the Shah's group] beat victims before arresting them." One voter, before leaving the polling place, was reported to have salaamed three times in the direction of the ballot box; asked why he had done so, he replied: "I am merely making my obeisance to the magic box. When one drops a ballot in for Mohammed [the ousted Premier Mossadegh], lo, when the box is opened, it is transformed into a vote for Fazdollah [the Shah's man]." [1]

THE EXTENT OF DIVERSITY

From what has been said so far, it is clear that in addition to patterns among governmental systems there is also a colorful (and sometimes dismaying) diversity, one which

---

[1] *New York Times*, March 11, 12, 1954.

is constantly increasing as more and more countries acquire their independence. Fifty years ago, there were less than fifty sovereign nations; today there are close to a hundred, with more soon to come. Some of these countries are still in the primitive stage of civilization, with nomadic forms of life and feudal, absolutistic institutions. Even within one region such as the Middle East, countries of this type, like Saudi Arabia and Yemen, lie close to advanced countries like Lebanon, with its sophisticated, commercial population, and Israel, with its high degree of organization in every aspect of life. Moreover, the degree of control may range all the way from government regulation and organization of almost everything to a bare minimum of government and administration in the operational sense. For example, in 1951, organized government in Syria (now part of the United Arab Republic) temporarily ceased to function: the cabinet had resigned and ceased to operate, and government officials had gone on strike. But nothing catastrophic, in fact nothing whatsoever, happened. Life went on as before, unaffected by this idyllic interlude of anarchy. The *New York Times* reported on August 6, 1951:

> Few people noticed that the entire administrative system of the Republic, together with the Government, had been out of action. What the situation amounted to was a demonstration of how superficial in many ways modern state institutions are in this part of the world. The age-old society that had carried on through wars and catastrophes simply went along as usual.

But while this was possible in a region where at that time feudalism still provided the bulk of the people with known and accepted rules of behavior, such a condition would, of course, create chaos in an industrial society based on far-reaching division of labor.

Finally, to mention one further diversity, there are countries which are formally independent but which only function economically, as well as politically and administratively, with the aid of foreign experts who, as advisers or employees of the indigenous government, actually run the country. Lybia, for instance, when established under United Nations auspices in 1951 as an independent country of federal and monarchical structure, possessed only a handful of its own people who had the training to fill any position in government and administration, while in mid-1960, the tragic case of the Congo re-emphasized the gap between need and human resources, between formal independence and actual viability. Under such circumstances, it may make little difference, at least initially, whether the form of government is democratic or authoritarian, monarchical or republican, unitary or federal.

THE TREND TOWARD UNIFORMITY

But despite all this, we should not exaggerate the factor of diversity. Behind the impression of great variety is a trend toward greater uniformity. Even though the impact of Western ideas and institutions has not (or not yet) been able to "modernize" (in Western terms) the actual political structure and life of many countries which have adopted an outwardly Western constitution or similar façade, most of them are beginning to modernize their economic structure, in particular to industrialize themselves in order to attain higher standards of living.

In the face of this trend toward modernization, the more traditionalist types of government, such as feudal and absolutist monarchies, inevitably decline. Traditionalism itself is bound to give way when the "revolution of rising expectations," with its demands for the better life which can be expected from scientific thought and industrial technology, penetrates areas in which fatalism had hitherto made people shun ideas of change and transformation. Once the expectation of rapid change is aroused, it cannot be stopped by inherited political institutions. Nothing, perhaps, distinguishes our age more sharply from preceding ages than the rate at which change is taking place. While populations are increasing at a fantastic rate and the number of independent countries is constantly growing, there is at the same time an ever-increasing interdependence among nations, arising out of mutual exploitation of resources, growing specialization of functions and, perhaps above all, the awareness that all countries, even the most powerful, are at the mercy of the appalling destructiveness of atomic and hydrogen weapons.

While it is obvious that traditional and feudal forms of government will steadily be overborne by economic change and particularly by industrialism, it is far from sure that this development will lead these countries toward more democratic forms of government. There was a time when we took it for granted that an advanced industrial country would be a democracy, but experience in the interwar period and since the end of World War II has undermined this belief. Totalitarianism, fascist or Communist, made deep inroads in that period into regions where democracy seemed firmly established or seemed at least to have a chance.

The trend toward uniformity, then, is not toward a single model or blueprint for political organization; rather it is toward either of two opposing models—the democratic and the totalitarian Communist—or toward some less easily characterized middle forms which, however, lean toward one or the other. It is time now to examine with some care the framework of limited government, the channels of political action, the role of executives, administration, and pressure groups, and the impact of belief systems and of international relations before we can come to more general conclusions about the prospects of democracy in an increasingly integrating and yet divided world.

IV

THE FRAMEWORK OF LIMITED GOVERNMENT

ORIGINS AND FUNCTIONS OF CONSTITUTIONS

Constitutions define, and thereby limit, public power. The distinctive characteristics of a totalitarian dictatorship are the facts that the power exercised by its governing group is unlimited and unrestrained and that the authority of the regime extends into every aspect of the life of the individual—religious and cultural as well as economic and social. In contrast, the exercise of political power in a democracy is limited by a constitutional framework which protects certain areas of personal and group life from governmental interference and provides that governmental powers shall be exercised in accordance with known procedures. The distinction between the two forms of government is basically, therefore, that between limited and unlimited government.

Genuine constitutions determining these limitations can

exist therefore only in nontotalitarian countries. Formal appearances notwithstanding, totalitarian regimes do not have them. At best, such regimes may enjoy merely a self-limitation on the part of the ruling group. And in any case, whatever rules exist are forever provisional, changeable, revocable; they do not have the nature of generality, reliability, and thus calculability which the rules of law elsewhere possess. Genuine constitutionalism is likewise absent where constitutions are forever made and remade, changed and abolished, so as to fit the political needs of the respective power-holders, as is all too often true in Latin-American countries.

There were times, in premodern ages, when constitutional rules delimiting the power of rulers were likewise absent. Yet such rule, even when it was presumed to be by divine right, was not totalitarian, since it was generally felt that rulers operated under a religious, moral, or natural law which was supposed to bind ruler and ruled alike. Thus the problem of political theory and practice was pre-eminently a personal one: how to educate the prince, for instance, so that he would govern for the common good. With the rise of the modern territorial state, however, and its impersonal and bureaucratic ordering of many spheres, government became too complicated to depend solely on the personal equation. Reliance was then put on the formulation and formalization of rules.

This does not imply that a constitution is always a written document which was adopted at a particular moment in history as a comprehensive regulation of governmental life. The British Constitution developed gradually, and largely in the form of custom. Yet what made the result of this process a constitution in the modern sense of the word was the fact that it not only defined but *limited* the power of the governing agencies. In the absence of this limiting function, the collections of rules and customs which during this same period—the later Middle Ages and early modern times—defined the arrangements of other political units did not form constitutions in this same sense.

Modern written constitutions arose in the past either from "pact" or from "compact." They arose from *pact* where, as in Continental Europe, they resulted from the contest between popular movements and royal absolutism over a share in political power. Thus, in the typical case of the Continental "constitutional monarch" of the nineteenth century, a written constitution would formalize a compromise between the crown and the people, or the crown and the estates, under which the previously unlimited power of the crown was now formally restrained. They arose from *compact* where, as in the United States, Canada, and Australia, nations were established under commonly agreed-upon rules, the "higher law" under which the people now vowed to live.

Even to this day, most constitutions reflect one or the other of these origins. In the first case, that of pact, the chief function of a constitution is likely to be the delimitation of the spheres of social classes, economic groups, castes, or other groups. In the case of compact, the chief importance of the constitution is as the symbol of unity, since it integrated the nation into one political unit. The delimitation of the spheres of power in this latter type of situation is between institutions which perform distinctive tasks—e.g., legislative and judicial—rather than between historically entrenched groups. The delimitation may also be between territorial divisions and the nation—i.e., federalism—but this rests also on the original and basic agreement of the whole people on how they shall be governed.

Sometimes constitutions having their origin in pact subsequently turn into compact, as in the case of Great Britain, where the original Constitution (in this case, a mixture of written and unwritten but accepted rules) first determined the partition of power between the King and nobles, and then between Crown and Parliament, but finally came to reflect the consensus under which the British people rule themselves. In this case, the sense for constitutionalism—i.e., abiding by rules which determine the allocations and use of political power—is joined to the sense of national unity. On the other hand, where, as in Germany, the basis for the original pact has disappeared and later constitutions have failed to attain the symbolic character which the Constitution has in the United States, constitutionalism remains fragile. This is equally the case in the new countries which are becoming independent before a national sentiment of unity has developed and which may be more concerned, at least initially, with economic and social advance than with recognizing the limits written into, or implicit in, their inherited structures of government.

The wide variations in the origins, functions, and strengths of constitutionalism can be illustrated by considering two of its most common and crucial characteristics: the system of fundamental rights and liberties, which embodies some of the most important substantive limitations on power; and constitutional jurisdiction, i.e., action through the courts to secure the observance of the rules of a constitution.

BASIC RIGHTS AND LIBERTIES TODAY

Perhaps the outstanding early statement of the fundamental rights and liberties of the citizen is embodied in the American Bill of Rights. But this and similar lists of rights have sometimes been criticized in this century as being too individualistic, too little concerned with the needs of groups, and too negative—in the sense of emphasizing "freedom from" rather than "freedom to." This last charge reflects the feeling that free speech and the protection against arbitrary search and seizure are small comfort to men who are denied the chance to earn a living and to improve their way of life. Whether the ordering of values implicit in such a charge is as self-evident today as it seemed in the interwar period is perhaps open to question. But in any case, it is true that catalogues of fundamental rights, not only in the sense of protection against government action but in other areas—such as the right to work and to decent payment for work, to social security, to education, and other rights characteristic of the welfare state—have been inserted not only in spurious documents like the Stalin Constitution, but also in modern democratic constitutions, i.e., the Weimar Constitution of Germany and the preambles to the Constitutions of the postwar Fourth French Republic and the Republic of India.

To the extent that they express the aspirations of underprivileged groups or classes or of underdeveloped nations, the importance of these latter rights is very great. Under such circumstances they can become the clarion calls of political movements, and their political impact may be greater than that of the "old-fashioned" freedoms. The Asian and African masses are often said to be more interested in freedom from want than in more rarefied concepts like freedom of opinion; though even if this is partially true, most of their leaders, at least, would prefer to combine both.

But the classical individual rights and freedoms retain

their value and even gain new luster when people have had the bitter experience of living under totalitarian or authoritarian rule. The loss of freedom makes us appreciate what we too easily take for granted as long as we have it. Life under totalitarian lawlessness teaches people anew the importance of basic personal freedoms, particularly that of legal security in its most elementary sense of freedom from arbitrary arrest and detention. It is significant that the Bonn Constitution has dropped most of the Weimar catalogue of economic and social rights while giving the traditional bill of rights new emphasis.

There are also some new departures in the sphere of the classical freedoms themselves. It is not surprising that in an age of mass society, emphasis should shift somewhat from the traditional political rights to those affecting personal development and cultural expression. Since individuals in a mass society must conform to the standards of mass organization and also must inevitably have less influence over policy decisions, the meaning of freedom is now also related to the right to nonconformity in those areas of life which have not yet been invaded by the state. Thus, in the United States, there has of late been interesting debate concerning the protection of the rights of creative expression in the arts, literature, and the entertainment fields; of the right to be protected against the too pervasive noise of one's environment; of the right of audiences to refuse to become "captive" victims of advertising; and of the right of the citizen, in a shrinking and integrated world, to move freely not only within his own country but in the world abroad, i.e., freely to leave and re-enter his country.

But the chief field of basic rights remains that of the classical bills of rights. Through these, from the time of "the mother of them all," the English Bill of Rights, there have been established not only the basic boundary lines of freedom, but also a bridge between liberalism and democracy, since without guarantees of some fundamental civil and political rights—the right to vote, freedom of speech, association, assembly, and the press, as well as freedom from arbitrary arrest and the right to *habeas corpus*, that is, to have your case reviewed publicly before a judge within a limited period of time after arrest—genuine democracy, in the sense of rule of the people, would be impossible. What is the present status of these rights in the major countries?

Not much need be said about the Soviet Union, where the famous Bill of Rights of the Stalin Constitution throughout the Stalinist era was merely a fig leaf for a dictatorship which, like all modern nondemocratic regimes, seemed unable to dispense with pseudodemocratic trappings. Of what avail are any of the classical freedoms if they may be exercised only "in conformity with the interests of the working people"—with this conformity defined only by the politically ruling group? Not yet have we had evidence of genuine guarantees of these "rights," either upheld in the courts, or acting as restrictions on the Soviet leaders.

The way in which rights and liberties are protected in the United States lies at the opposite pole from the practice in the Soviet Union. Even as compared with other liberal democratic systems, the American system is more fully defined and seems more safely implemented and protected. Rights and liberties are written into both federal and state constitutions, which enjoy the aura of a "higher law." They are protected not only against executive but also against legislative infringement; and independent courts function so as to make observation and enforcement real.

But even in the United States, under the impact of strains and stresses (for instance, those of bipolarity and the cold war), limits to these rights have become apparent. Some of these limits are necessary. The ingenious strategies of modern totalitarian movements confront democracies with the dilemma of whether to grant unlimited freedom to their enemies who would use it to destroy freedom for others, or whether to restrict freedom and risk a too far-reaching curtailment, or at least a dangerous erosion, of liberties. In tending toward the second alternative, the United States has permitted a lessening of political rights by recognizing certain legal limitations of liberties, in particular through a broad construction of the "clear-and-present-danger" test. Without the same justification, and far more dangerous, however, are the extralegal social pressures for conformity. Experience of the latter, especially in the period of the McCarthy investigations, shows how dependent are formal guarantees upon public support.

Yet, if fear and pressure for conformism threatened basic rights for this period of time in the United States, Great Britain offers us encouraging evidence on the other side, that is, that continued respect for freedom is itself the best guarantee of basic rights. The preservation of traditional liberties in that country provides a prime illustration of the force of tradition and the prevailing spirit of a nation, as contrasted with the impact of formal rules and institutions. Even though no higher law of a written constitution protects the basic rights of an Englishman, they are safely guarded through the application of the rule of law. While Parliament, by legislation, or the Cabinet, by delegated power, clearly has the power to tamper with personal rights, there is little danger that either would do so more than temporarily, and then only during genuine emergencies. So closely is Britain integrated as a nation of free men mutually tolerant and respectful of their differences that, in Churchill's words, they can "lump" (i.e. swallow, or accept) the most unpleasant of such divergencies. Typical of this attitude was Churchill's comment on the opinions and activities of Hewlett Johnson, the "Red Dean" of Canterbury: "Free speech carries with it the evils of all the foolish, unpleasant, venomous things that are said, but on the whole we would rather lump them than do away with them."

Even Britain, however, politically mature though it is, has its frailties, more noticeable abroad than at home. To the British, basic rights have always been rights of Englishmen rather than the rights of man. Though the native people of their colonial possessions have received genuine blessings, like the extension of the common law, impartial standards of administration, and sound rules of hygiene and health, they have not often enjoyed until late in their development either the political rights or the tolerance of unpopular opinions which are among Britain's most distinguished attributes at home.

In contrast to the British, the French since the age of the Enlightenment and the Great Revolution have raised the battle cry of the "rights of man," rather than the rights of Frenchmen. But the trouble has been that it was the battle cry of only one group of Frenchmen in the perennial French conflict of opposing ideologies. Many a glorious legal and political battle has been fought over these rights and their protection, and some of them have been decisive for the liberal democratic development of the country—as witness the Dreyfus affair, where a long and ultimately successful fight was waged at the turn of the century to clear the name of an unjustly convicted Jewish army officer. But it can hardly be said that these rights are as safely anchored in France as they are in Britain. The French system is at its best in the protection it offers of individual liberties through its system of administrative jurisdiction, but these procedures protect personal rights, such as property rights, against an entrenched and solid bureaucracy, rather than political freedoms. It would be gratifying to infer from the broad freedoms enjoyed in France by political movements of even the most radical sort, including Communism, a British-type agreement on "lumping it" in the interests of freedom and diversity; what seems more likely, however, is that this freedom was the result of dissent and of the weakness of the public power, which asserted itself with difficulty in the face of warring factions.

As for Germany, there as in France liberalism has not been unsuccessful in the realm of personal security and property rights; these were clearly protected by that Central European marriage of freedom and authoritarianism known as the *Rechtsstaat*. But political rights and liberties prior to the republican regime of Weimar meant little more than futile ventilation of grievances in press or parliament, to which the ruling powers paid scant attention. If the Weimar regime distinguished—and perhaps extinguished—itself through an overly broad grant of political freedoms, the Bonn Constitution also experiments in two novel and interesting ways: first, by declaring that certain especially fundamental rights are unamendable (Article 79), a provision which raises the difficult problem of whether there can and should be limits to the power of constitutional amendment; and second, by setting out limits upon the exercise of political rights when used "in order to attack the liberal-democratic order" (Articles 18, 21). It was under these latter provisions that neo-Nazis and later the Communist Party were suppressed in West Germany.

The suppression of the Communist Party in certain countries brings sharply into focus a problem which troubles many democratic states: what to do about organized Communist activity in their political life and in their trade unions. In Italy and France, of course, the Communist Party remains not only legal but capable of attracting large numbers of votes; it also retains a strong, even dominant, influence in the trade unions. In Great Britain, no one would suggest action against the small Communist Party which continues, election after election, to put up candidates, though with uniform lack of success. There has been much more concern about the strong and pervasive Communist influence in some British trade unions, but the problem has been left to the unions themselves, which ultimately succeeded in limiting its scope. Particularly interesting in this regard is the experience of Australia, whose Liberal administration was returned to office in 1951, largely on a platform of making the Communist Party illegal, an end sought not because the party was strong politically, but because of its dominance within powerful trade unions. The legislation which was passed for this purpose was declared unconstitutional by the courts, and the effort was subsequently abandoned. As in Great Britain, however, the Australian unions thereafter made a substantial and largely successful effort to rid themselves of Communist control.

More direct attacks on local Communist Parties have been carried out in Canada, the United States, and South Africa. Canada outlawed its Communist Party in the early thirties, but has not acted against the small Labour Progressive Party which took its place. The United States has extended the clear-and-present-danger test, as we have said, and has used the Smith Act of 1940 to prosecute successfully over one hundred prominent Communist Party leaders on the charge of advocating the overthrow of government by force. Moreover, the Communist Control Act of 1954 prevents the Communist Party from operating, at least in the federal sphere, as a legal entity, i.e., from putting candidates on a ballot or suing in court. But the American Communist Party has not yet been formally outlawed, so that it may be said to exist in a quasi-legal form.

Most far-reaching of such measures is South Africa's Suppression of Communism Act (1950), which made unlawful not only the Communist Party, but any other organization said to promote Communistic activities. Under the law, there is a liquidator who is empowered to take over the assets of such organizations and to compile a list of their officeholders or supporters. These persons can then be publicly named and thereafter forbidden by the Minister to take part in any specified organization, to enter or remain in a prescribed area, or to attend any gathering of more than three persons.

It has become clear from the administration of this South African Act that many people other than registered Communist Party members can be attacked under its provisions. The Act defines Communism not only as the doctrine of Marxian Socialism expounded by Lenin or Trotsky or any other doctrine which seeks to establish a one-party state based on the dictatorship of the proletatriat, but also as any scheme "which aims at bringing about any political, industrial, social, or economic change within the Union by the promotion of disturbances or disorder, by unlawful acts or omissions. . . ." When this latter provision was used to convict the leaders of the non-white passive disobedience campaign in 1952, the judge termed their offense "statutory Communism." Thus, it is all too apparent how far such provisions can be made to go. Two white members of Parliament, both elected as native representatives by the small African electorate in Cape Province (since 1960 no longer permitted representation in the House of Assembly) lost their seats, and another former Communist was prevented from standing for office; numerous trade-union leaders were removed from their offices; and almost all the articulate non-white leaders have been placed under ban at one time or another. Few situations point out more clearly the dangers implicit in such broadly worded statutes. Nor is there much evidence here, or elsewhere, that a ban on the Communist Party does much more than drive its activities underground.

Such a survey as this underlines the fact with which we started—that the response to Communist infiltration and the pressures of the international situation may threaten to erode the protection of traditional and fundamental civil and political rights. In a country like South Africa, where the white minority is outnumbered four to one by the non-whites, the fear of Communist influence easily becomes intermingled with the potential threat of African nationalism. Even in the United States, and in spite of the formal guarantees of its Bill of Rights, individuals have been convicted and imprisoned on the basis of what they are said to advocate, rather than of specific acts which they have committed. To safeguard individual rights in the light of such pressures requires not only restraint on the part of government, but also constant alertness by the governed.

CONSTITUTIONAL JURISDICTION

It is common in democratic countries to look on the courts not only as the protectors of individual rights, but also as the agency which ensures that state action will not transgress constitutional limits. "Constitutional jurisdiction," as we have said, means court action to secure the observance of the rules of a constitution. As such, it may attain political importance far beyond that of any other judicial action.

It is hardly surprising that constitutional jurisdiction has been particularly important in countries with a federal structure, such as the United States, Canada, Australia, Switzerland, West Germany, and Austria. Delimiting the powers of member units in relation to those of the federal (national) unit is vital for the functioning of such a system. It took a civil war in the United States to establish the principle that a judicial organ of the federal government, rather than an individual state (or states) is the final arbiter. As resistance to the Supreme Court decision in the school segregation cases points up, this principle has to be re-established again and again. Ultimately, history has shown that such delimitations of power depend not only on judicial interpretation, but also on acquiescence by the most powerful forces in a community in the decisions which have been made.

The different ways in which constitutional jurisdiction functions can be illustrated by the experience of three countries where such jurisdiction has assumed major importance: Switzerland, West Germany, and the United States. There are three chief areas in which courts[1] may undertake to guarantee the functioning of a constitutional system, and each of the countries mentioned illustrates one of them. In the first place, the courts may act to up-

---

[1] Whether constitutional jurisdiction is exercised by the general courts of a country (as in the United States and in Switzerland) or by a special and separate "constitutional tribunal" (as in Germany, Austria, and Italy) is immaterial in this connection.

hold the individual or group rights and liberties which a constitution protects. A second important sphere is the relation between ordinary legislation and the law of the constitution. The third is to keep in balance both the powers of, and the relations between, organs of government, e.g., the spheres of the legislature and executive, the rights of majorities and minorities in a parliament, or the jurisdiction of the federal government and the member states. Accordingly, constitutional jurisdiction may deal with any or all of the following: (a) conflicts between the state and individuals or groups wherein the latter claim there has been a violation of basic rights or liberties; (b) judicial review of the constitutionality of laws; (c) "organ conflicts," that is, conflicts between the organs of the state or government.

The Swiss system chiefly implements point *a* above. There is in Switzerland no court decision in organ conflicts, and there is no judicial review of federal (in contrast to cantonal) statutes. The chief function of Swiss constitutional jurisdiction, therefore, is the broad protection of individual and group rights in cases of the "constitutional complaint" of citizens. This function reflects a profound concern with the maintenance of a sphere of individual freedom from state interference. In contrast, the distinctive function of the American judicial system (though not, to be sure, its only function, since that system is also concerned with the protection of rights and liberties) is judicial review (point *b* above), i.e., the maintenance of the superiority of the Constitution over all state action, including ordinary lawmaking. This reflects an ingrained American feeling that the Constitution is the higher law, to be preserved against the changing and possibly transitory will of the people.

The new German system, finally, is perhaps most interesting in providing for legal settlement of organ conflicts (point *c*). The idea of offering political groups and governmental authorities a chance to fight out constitutional conflicts legally perhaps reflects a typically German legalistic approach to political problems generally. Moreover, it goes back to the nineteenth-century origin of Continental constitutions in the crown vs. people compromise. Even under the German Empire (when the *Bundesrat,* the upper chamber, had jurisdiction), and later under Weimar (when a constitutional tribunal was established), provision had been made for the resolution of certain types of organ conflicts. But only now has full "juridification" of the system been attained, with the Bonn Constitution allotting to the Federal Constitutional Court the power to decide even those constitutional conflicts which arise among the highest federal organs and agencies, such as, for instance, between the government and a parliamentary opposition group over the enactment of a law. Here, as well as in the protection of rights and liberties and through judicial review, the new German Constitutional Court has vigorously asserted itself. This, for a country with strong authoritarian traditions, is an important new venture.

What about constitutional jurisdiction in other countries and systems? Totalitarian regimes, of course, cannot permit procedures for the effective limitation of power; they avoid even the make-believe appearance of such jurisdictions, asserting that to give courts powers of judicial review, for instance, would hamstring the sovereign legislature. While in totalitarian systems this attitude simply reflects the determination to keep all power in the hands of the sovereign ruling group, the party, it is also true that the French have used the same argument in all sincerity. To the French, who traditionally believed that sovereignty rested inalienably in the people and its elected assembly, the idea of a higher law of the Constitution is foreign. Their unitary system leaves no room for federal-state conflicts; nor is there any possibility of judicial review of national legislation or of a judicial decision of organ conflicts. But it would be strange, indeed, to find no institutional protection of individual rights in the very country of the *droits de l'homme et du citoyen;* and we do find such protection in the system of administrative jurisdiction, headed by the *Conseil d'État* (Council of State), which takes infinite care to protect individuals from unjust or unfair acts committed by government officials or in the name of the state. French administrative jurisdiction, in fact, not only provides redress for private citizens in situations in which Anglo-Saxon law does not recognize public responsibility—for example being injured by a bullet fired by the police at an escaping bandit—but also accepts the obligation of the state to pay for the mistakes of its employees if they cause damage to property—e.g., destroying a cow in the mistaken belief it has foot-and-mouth disease—where Anglo-Saxon law assumes only personal responsibility and necessitates a civil suit.

The British system of parliamentary supremacy, like the French system, is innocent of judicial review or judicial settlement of organ conflicts. It is typically British in avoiding the use of special institutions for protection and in relying, instead, on such general rules and traditions as the rule of law, the recognition of implied restraints upon state power, and the application of the rule of reason to any and all of the system's manifestations. Thus again, Britain illustrates the importance, beyond constitutional procedures and institutional devices, of national tradition for the maintenance of a constitutionalism which is nowhere more safely anchored than in that country.

INDEPENDENCE OF THE JUDICIARY

Constitutional jurisdiction is not the only device for safeguarding constitutionalism. There is also an essential relationship between constitutionalism and the judicial function in general. The decisive factor here is judicial independence, whose general importance for the maintenance of a democratic system has already been noted. In contrast to police states, where the courts are looked on as instruments of the regime in carrying out its political and general purposes, courts in constitutional systems are separate, independent agencies, bound by their own rules of procedure and determining cases according to publicly known law.

It is through judicial independence (usually guaranteed by the appointment of judges for life or until a certain age, and their irremovability except for moral causes) that Montesquieu's device for the limitation of power has found its last redoubt in countries like Great Britain and France, where little else remains of the separation of powers. Under modern conditions of the welfare state and of government regulation, the separation between the lawmaking and the executive branches may no longer be as feasible or even as desirable as it used to be; but the separation of an independent judiciary from both seems to be the irreducible minimum required for an effective system of limitation of power. The more modern government interferes, administers, and regulates, the more urgent is the need to preserve a check on the way these activities affect individuals and groups. The helplessness of the individual in the absence of such control is all too obvious in systems where the judiciary is either dependent or powerless, whether they be premodern systems with their *lettres de cachet,* or modern totalitarian systems with their knock on the door in the dead of night.

Modern tyranny has given a new perspective to the old charges that bourgeois justice is liable to dispense class justice. British socialists, for instance, used to claim that the British judicial system and the common law itself gave particular advantages to the claims of property. But no longer are such charges often heard. For one thing, British courts placed no impediments in the way of Labour's programs after 1945. But far more important has been the terrifying example of those trials in Nazi Germany, the Soviet Union, and the Soviet satellites in which the law has been deliberately twisted to entrap the defendant and judges have acted as prosecutors and executioners rather than as impartial umpires. In the face of such experience, the independence of the judiciary, known processes of law, and the continuity of principles underlying legal decisions have taken on new importance.

Democracies nevertheless still have their problems. Equal justice under law must, after all, be dispensed by men. The government of laws must forever be government by people applying and interpreting the laws. And human beings, however strong their feeling of independence and security, inevitably have preferred ideals and predilections, and even preconceived ideas and prejudices. An aging judiciary may be behind the times; a judiciary drawn from certain strata or classes may well reflect some caste or class bias. To some extent, and in the long run, even the United States Supreme Court "follows the election returns," and while this is reasonable if it means no more than paying attention in a general way to what the people want, it could be dangerous if it led to the abridgment of basic liberties. Moreover, the law itself necessarily reflects class interest where there is class rule, economic interests where such interests prevail in a given society, religious interests where particular denominations or churches predominate. The remedy here, if one is desired, is not a change in the judicial system but a change in the laws through democratic processes. As for class, personal, or any other bias of the judicial personnel, the remedy is not to render the judiciary more dependent, but constantly to bring about reforms that make such shortcomings less likely, for example, selecting the German and even the British judiciary from a less narrow class base and protecting the American judiciary, especially on the state level, from undue party influence such as is apt to result from the election of judges for limited terms.

Entrusting courts with the authority to limit the use of power by other governmental agencies creates certain problems. Difficulties arise, for instance, where courts are entrusted with overly political tasks. When, as in the United States, courts are called upon to decide broad issues involving free enterprise versus governmental regulation or racial segregation versus integration through the interpretation of constitutional norms containing general terms like "due process of law" or "equal protection of the laws," decisions are bound to go beyond the realm of ordinary interpretation and to involve elements of policy-making. Recognizing this fact, the practice of many countries is to consider certain political questions (such as particular foreign policy issues in American practice, or *actes de gouvernement,* as in France) as nonjusticiable, that is, as falling outside the jurisdiction of the courts. Of course, decisions in such cases have to be made somewhere. Whether ultimate control is given to a judicial body or to the more political part of the government which is in charge of the particular field seems to be a matter of tradition and convenience. There are both problems and advantages, whichever way the matter is handled. Allowing an independent judiciary to settle such issues may create the danger of rendering the judiciary open to charges of being political; but it may offer protection against the concentration or abuse of power elsewhere. Leaving the decision with an executive or a parliament does provide more concentration of authority; but it may be argued that this is the more democratic method, especially where the executive or assembly has a direct mandate from the electorate.

Another problem arises when constitutions undertake to render any and all constitutional conflicts justiciable, that is, to be settled by the courts. The more encompassing the range of what is considered justiciable, the greater the danger that in a conflict involving basic issues of policy or fundamentally opposed forces in state and society, normative judgments will prove unenforceable. It is during those crises of a regime or country which test the very bases of its institutions that constitutionalism is put to its real test. Only a civil war, and not the Supreme Court, could resolve the issues of slavery and of state sovereignty in the United States. The Constitutional Court of Weimar Germany was equally unable to enforce its verdict (compromise decision though it was) when antidemocratic forces undertook to destroy the last stronghold of Weimar democracy. Everything depends in such cases on whether judicial bodies are backed up by sufficiently strong public determination to uphold the rule of law in this broader sense.

The crucial importance of a sense of restraint on the

part of governing groups is well illustrated by the highly complex situation which developed in South Africa over the Nationalist Government's attempts to place on a separate voting roll the Cape Coloured, the last group of non-whites which was still permitted to vote for the same candidates as did whites. Basing their action on a legal technicality of some subtlety, the Nationalists tried to achieve this purpose through ordinary legislation, though the South African Constitution[1] provided that the voting rights of non-whites in the Cape should not be changed except by a two-thirds majority of both chambers meeting in joint session. The immediate opposition to this attempt gave rise to a spontaneous nationwide organization called the Torch Commando, which attacked the inherent unconstitutionality of the Nationalist approach regardless of whether it might be upheld in the courts. When the South African Court of Appeal declared the legislation invalid, the opposition's view was confirmed. But the Nationalists refused to accept the verdict as a final settlement of the issue and, again by a simple majority, passed an act providing for a High Court of Parliament. This body, which was to consist of the entire membership of Parliament, was to take over from the Appeal Court the power to review legislation; in effect this meant that the Parliament assumed the right to validate its own legislation. The opposition members in Parliament thereupon refused to participate in the High Court of Parliament, and the

---

[1] The South African Constitution is the South Africa Act (1909) passed by the British Parliament but drafted by South Africans themselves. The same is true of the Canadian and Australian Constitutions. Except for its entrenched clauses (that is, those providing for change only by a two-thirds vote of both the upper and lower chambers sitting together) the South Africa Act can be amended by simple majority action of the South African Parliament. The only entrenched clause now remaining safeguards the equality of the two official languages, Afrikaans and English.

Appeal Court declared this act to be invalid also, as it was clearly designed to serve the purpose of the earlier legislation.

Balked in this second attempt to take the Coloured off the common roll, the Nationalists proceeded to make the "sovereignty of Parliament" and the "interference" of the courts issues in the 1953 general election. Returned to power with an increased parliamentary majority, Dr. Malan then tried twice to secure a constitutional amendment placing the Coloured on a separate roll to elect representatives of their own, as Cape Africans had done since 1936. Since he was unable to win the necessary two-thirds majority in the House of Assembly and Senate, his successor, Mr. Strijdom, then moved to more stringent measures. Five new judges were added to the Appeal Court, and soon afterward a new measure raised the quorum to eleven whenever the court considers the validity of an act of Parliament. Still more startling was a measure to change the size, composition, and way of selecting the members of the Senate. The new second chamber, selected under this Act at the end of 1955, was increased from forty-eight to eighty-nine members, of whom the Nationalists controlled seventy-seven, as compared with thirty in the old chamber. These additions enabled the Nationalists in mid-1956 to pass their constitutional amendment to place the Coloured on a separate voting roll to select four whites to represent them in the House of Assembly.

Once again there were demonstrations against the "unconstitutionality" of the Nationalist action; a new movement, the Black Sash Women, sprang into existence and publicized its opposition by standing with bowed heads in mourning for the "dead" Constitution whenever a

Nationalist minister appeared. But none of these efforts was effective. Though English-speaking South Africans, in particular, were outraged by the Senate Act, they were not prepared to do more than to vote against it and to show their opposition by peaceful demonstrations. Even these tended to die down with time. The Torch Commando virtually went out of existence after the 1953 election, and the Black Sash Women are now rarely seen.

It became obvious in this situation that the Nationalists have no basic sense of constitutionality, such as sparked the vigorous American opposition to the relatively mild "court-packing" proposal of President Roosevelt in 1937, which would have added another judge to the Supreme Court whenever one of those already serving reached the age of 75. Even though he had achieved a remarkable electoral success the year before, Roosevelt felt obliged to bow to the storm of criticism evoked by this scheme and to withdraw it. But in the absence of such an attitude, demonstrations have little effect. Under these circumstances, the South African opposition to Nationalist expedients could have been effective only if it had been ready to resort to forcible measures, which might conceivably have led to a clash of arms. Natural reluctance to go so far was reinforced by the fact that in many quarters of the opposition there was little concern for the rights of the Coloured as such. Thus, lacking the sense of personal commitment to a group which was being deprived of its rights, and even perhaps to a Constitution which was a compromise between racial groups rather than a symbol of unity, the opposition ultimately acquiesced in the situation. By so doing, however, it left the way open for subsequent measures which imperil the rule of law. To lose the safeguard of established rules of procedure as limitations on the power of the parliamentary majority is to make possible the uncertainties of arbitrary rule.

DECONCENTRATION OF POWER

So far we have been considering the limits which are placed on government through the protection of individual rights, the restraints of the constitution, and the functional division of powers between the executive, legislature, and judiciary. It is now time to look in some detail at the territorial division of power, or at least of responsibility, which is provided by local government and by federalism. Historically, the limitations upon the authority of a central government which are imposed by deconcentration developed long before constitutional and legal limitations. The "absolute" monarchies of prerevolutionary Europe, for instance, were much less absolute in practice than they claimed to be in theory. This was simply because the central government was not then technically equipped to deal with local matters in remote parts of the country. Today, national government, and especially national administration, is so organized that it can and usually does operate side by side with the organs of local and of intermediate units of government even in the most remote places. In fact, the distinctive feature of a federation, in contrast to a confederation, is that national law is operative throughout the country. The expansion of national functions and responsibilities, however, endangers the functioning of those local, and possibly regional levels of government which used to enjoy virtual autonomy and thus removed whole areas from the influence of the central government.

LOCAL SELF-GOVERNMENT

Traditionally, one of the counterweights against too much centralized government was found in local self-government. It is often said, and with some justice, that the "grass roots" of democracy, its essential training ground, are to be found at the local level, where people deal with problems of immediate and direct importance to themselves—problems, moreover, which are intelligible to them in terms of their personal experience. Significantly, local government in Germany developed and was able to gain genuine importance at a time when German state institutions were still authoritarian; again, after the German collapse at the end of World War II, self-government first reasserted itself at the local level. Not only have local self-governing institutions shown stubborn vitality in times of stress; they can also provide a healthy counterbalance to overcentralization, restraining the "apoplexy at the center and the anemia at the extremities" which are always dangers in the highly organized, bureaucratic state of today.

It must be admitted, however, that even in countries with long traditions of local self-government, there is a marked trend toward looking on local government as a device for mere decentralization rather than as a counterbalance to the central administration. In Britain, for instance, many activities, such as education and public health, which used to be locally inspired are now organized on a national scale; genuine self-government on the local level thus threatens to become a casualty of the welfare state.

Yet there is still a marked difference between the British and American systems of local government and that of the French. In France, the authority of the prefect remains supreme within the department, the largest of the local divisions; but the prefect is the political agent of the central administration. In Britain and the United States, in contrast, local officials are employed and paid by the local units, even though in many cases they must meet nationally or state-imposed standards.

The most serious evidence of decline in the vitality of local government in many countries is the lack of interest in local issues. In France, Britain, and Germany, for instance, local elections are increasingly looked on as trials of strength for the national parties, which interject national issues into local contests. Although this somewhat increases public interest, it also entails the danger that political contests, like administrative programs, are merely being decentralized and have no firm roots in local needs. In this perspective, the localism of American politics may appear to have more merit than is commonly recognized.

FEDERALISM

Federalism is a much more effective means than local government of providing deconcentration of authority, since it establishes constitutional arrangements allocating power to the regional as well as to the national governments. One of the important functions of the constitutional jurisdiction of the courts in countries like the United States, Canada, Australia, Germany, Switzerland, or Nigeria, where a federal division of power exists, is to watch over the delimitation of the powers of both the central authority and the component units, as we have noted, and to afford protection to their continued existence and spheres of action whenever a relevant case raises the issue. Yet although this safeguard exists, the problems encountered in local government also appear to some extent where federalism provides an intermediary level of government between local and central affairs.

Even in the classical federal systems, whether in the largest or in one of the smallest democracies in the world—the United States and Switzerland—there is now a serious question whether units below the national government which are not mere administrative subdivisions of that government can effectively carry out more than strictly local functions in a period when so many activities are necessarily nationwide, if not even broader. Both national planning and national security are necessarily functions of the national government, and these activities tend to become ever more encompassing. Switzerland even formally amended its Constitution in 1947 in order to enlarge the jurisdiction of the federation in economic matters. The fact that only the federal government can command the resources to finance large-scale development programs and social welfare has greatly strengthened the position of the national administration in Australia and to a lesser, though still marked degree, in Canada. Thus, there is a marked trend toward centralism in the older, established federal systems of the world.

In the face of this development, students of federalism have given much thought to its inherent constitutional and political problems. There is a long series of classical problems of federalism. Should the federal or state sphere possess what unspecified residual powers there are? Should the administration of national laws be entrusted to national executive agencies, as in the United States, or should it be carried on in the main through state bureaucracies but under federal supervision, as in Germany and Switzerland? The same question arises, be it noted, in respect to the organization of the judiciary: Should there be, on the American pattern, two parallel columns of courts reaching from bottom to top in both the federal and the state spheres; or, as in Europe, Australia, and Canada, state judiciaries coordinated by one federal supreme court? Finally, there is the question of how best to organize that body which in federal structures customarily represents the member units on the federal level of government. Is it better to follow the American or Australian senatorial systems, where delegates to the second chamber are representatives of the people, and elected by their votes; or, as might seem theoretically closer to the idea of federalism, to have the delegates represent the state units, i.e., their governments, on the German pattern?

All of these questions in turn are influenced by broader underlying forces and trends. While, for instance, the unit which enjoys unlisted (i.e., underfined) residual powers might seem to have the advantage, the real balance depends on how broadly the listed ("enumerated") powers are in practice defined and applied. In Canada, where residual powers were vested in the central government, judicial decisions by the Privy Council long acted to build up the separate jurisdictions of the provinces. In contrast, American constitutional history serves to show how terms like "interstate commerce" may be used to enhance central power at the expense of the member units, despite the vesting of residual powers in the latter. What really counts is the viability of the member units, which today is determined by two major factors: the financial and the political.

The political factor resolves itself into the question of whether genuine and sufficiently strong social, economic, and cultural interests, possibly backed up by regionally concentrated nationality, linguistic, or religious groups, seek protection from centralization through reinforcing states' rights. Financial viability depends on the distribution of the chief financial resources, especially taxes. Even constitutional systems like the Australian and the German, which began by reserving most of the sources of income to the states, have ended by giving the federal government the major share of financial powers and resources. In countries like the United States, where, constitutionally, there is free competition between levels of government in tapping resources, the balance of income and expenditures has likewise shifted overwhelmingly to the national level.

Even more relevant than the financial factor to the survival and viability of federalism is whether or not strong sentiments of regionalism exist. There is in this respect a striking contrast between old-established systems, such as the United States and the European federal states, and the new countries of the world. In the old federal countries, with the possible exception of Canada and Switzerland, one gains the impression that strongly felt regionalism is largely obsolescent. As distances shrink in the air age, as metropolitan areas cut through state lines, and as people move like latter-day nomads from place to place, the traditionalist, partly nonrational, regional sentiment which underlies genuine federalism tends to diminish and, indeed, to atrophy.

It is nevertheless true in the older federal countries that certain interests which by themselves have little to do with regionalism have tried to underpin federal divisions. Thus, in Germany, national political parties find their control of state governments a vantage point from which to influence national policies. In Austria, the Social Democratic Party, whose doctrine is centralist rather than federalist, is strongly entrenched in the member unit of Vienna and for this reason defends the Austrian federal system; and so does its chief opponent, the People's Party, which controls the rural and Alpine states. In the United States, mining, gas, oil, or similar interests may become more influential by virtue of their dominant position in particular states and their consequent influence on those states' senators in Washington, and thus be more ardent supporters of federalism. The American party system as such, of course, is still built on local and regional organizations. But none of this evidences strong regional feelings among the people at large—feelings which do not in fact exist, except for white sectionalism in the South. Canada is somewhat different, partly because of French-speaking Quebec, partly because the provincial units are far larger and more distinctive than are American states. Canadian federalism has been reinforced not only by judicial interpretations, as we have seen, but also by the not-infrequent practice of the electorate of choosing different parties to control provincial administrations from those they support nationally—probably for the very purpose of maintaining some territorial checks and balances to powerful national parties.

Nonetheless, regardless of local situations, the issues represented by political parties in the older, established states are national, as, inevitably, are the interests and organizations of the chief social and economic groups (labor, trade, and industry) in industrial countries. This is probably the chief reason why the new federalism written into Italy's postwar Constitution has remained a dead letter, with the possible exception of two regions—Sicily and the (formerly Austrian) Alto Adige.

Only in regions such as the two just mentioned does federalism still seem to have some genuine regional backing in the sense of a feeling that nationality, language, or general historical background sets them apart from other groups or from the majority population. The basis for the different status of Scotland and Wales in Britain (which, of course, is not federalism) is not entirely dissimilar. Quebec in Canada, Bavaria in Germany, Catalonia and the Basque regions in Spain before the Franco dictatorship did away with their autonomy, reflect the same distinctiveness. But with industrialization, even these differences are gradually being overlaid.

Thus the outlook for federalism in the older systems is none too good. But this does not necessarily provide a danger for liberalism. It is far from sure that smaller units of government are more sensitive to the rights and liberties of individuals and groups than are larger ones. Moreover, against the pressure of nongovernmental power, such as that of "big business" or any other big interest group, central government sometimes provides more effective protection. In any event, some kind of administrative decentralization will undoubtedly be retained in many spheres of activity in order to lessen the load on national administrations.

If, in the democracies, federal divisions are becoming less important, in the dictatorships they are simply irrelevant. Although the Soviet Union is technically a federation, the division of power is far more apparent than real. Responsibilities in Khrushchev's Russia are shared between the national and regional spheres much more than they were under Stalin. But the essential characteristics of the Soviet as of the Nazi system demand the concentration of power in one man or in a small group backed by a monolithic party which permeates all operations throughout the country. In Latin America, too, federalism (largely copied from the United States), is often simply make-believe, even where there is no dictatorship. Its general weakness is reflected in the easy use of "federal intervention," which substitutes federal for regional control in the member units.

On the other hand, federalism seems to have particular importance in the world today in nations which have only recently, or are about to, come into existence. When large units gain their independence from colonial rule, federalism may be the only way to prevent their disintegration into nonviable linguistic or similar fragments. India, whose federalism now reflects its great range of linguistic groups, retained its unity only by yielding to their demands for separate divisions. The trend toward further subdivisions may, however, call forth a counteracting trend, with centralism enforced in the interests of maintaining unity. This happened in Indonesia, which was transformed from a federation into a centralized republic soon after gaining independence.

Federalism may be the best way, moreover, by which otherwise too small units can group themselves into viable entities. The United States provides the earliest illustration of this process. The Canadian and the Australian colonies also took this route to national unity and statehood between 1867 and 1901. That South Africa, in contrast, selected a unitary system (with substantial, but not guaranteed, responsibilities for its provinces) is now seen in the perspective of Afrikaner Nationalist domination to have enabled a slim Afrikaans-speaking national white majority to impose disliked policies (e.g., in education) on largely English-speaking Natal. A more evenly balanced allocation of powers between its three units—Southern Rhodesia, Northern Rhodesia, and Nyasaland—and the central government might have provided the Federation of Rhodesia and Nyasaland, established in 1953, with more political stability to complement its economic growth, though the key issue, as in South Africa, is to find a reasonable balance between the power of the dominant white minority and the legitimate demands of African nationalism. In newly independent Nigeria, with half the population of West Africa, federalism has proved capable of holding together three widely differing regions, each with a dominant tribal group: Yoruba in the West, Ibo in the East, and Hausa-Fulani in the numerically predominant North. As in the early days of Canada and Australia, the need of Nigeria's regionally based political parties to reach into other areas or combine with outside groups if they are to achieve national power not only limits separatism, but also creates a healthy balance of forces which could underpin constitutionalism. The Malayan Federation, another recent addition to the independent members of the Commonwealth of Nations, is a further example of the advantages of the federal form in combining self-conscious smaller units. The West Indian Federation has not yet overcome the separatism of its widely dispersed units and, like the Federation of Rhodesia and Nyasaland, will not achieve independence and Commonwealth membership unless or until its units develop a soundly based sense of the advantages of unity. Thus, federalism is seen to provide a framework for experimentation and a flexibility in determining the allocation of power which can make its form suitable to widely varying conditions.

If federalism can play this role in the making of new nations and thus provide the middle way between splinter units and excessive centralization, it may yet come to play an even larger role in international relations. The increasing interdependence of countries in the field of security and the growing economic integration of the world may, in the long run, suggest the value of a federal relation to countries with small resources and extensive needs of development. This would be particularly appropriate in West Africa, Equatorial Africa, and East Africa, where the breakneck race for independence has brought and is bringing a large number of small countries to a political status which their immature economies cannot support. Not only these new countries of Africa, but possibly far older ones, too, may recognize the value of a federal relationship, now that they are obviously too ineffective internationally to do more than exist in the shadow of larger ones. The more audacious might look forward to seeing federalism used as a device to integrate even the major powers whose basis of genuine independence has disappeared along with their former "impenetrable" frontiers, and perhaps even to seeing, in the far distant future, a world federal structure.

V

CHANNELS OF POLITICAL ACTION: ELECTIONS, POLITICAL PARTIES, AND LEGISLATURES

Although constitutions form the framework within which governments should operate, they cannot of themselves answer the most vital question for a democratic state: How is government to be kept responsive to the popular will? It is still possible in a New England town meeting to bring together the citizens to make their own decisions on policy, as Athenians used to do in classical times. But national populations are far too large and too dispersed in modern times for such direct action (even though the device of a national plebiscite is occasionally used, as in Switzerland in the legislative process or in Australia in the process of constitutional amendment). Modern government thus is representative government. But this very fact raises a vast number of other questions: How are representatives to be chosen so that they will be responsible to their constituents? How can they make their influence effective on the executive? In other words, how can the vast variety of often opposing groups in a modern community be linked effectively with the process of government in such a way that policy-making can be carried on speedily and decisively and yet with due regard to the consent of the governed?

THE PROCESS AND PURPOSE OF ELECTIONS

The most obvious point at which citizens directly influence the conduct of government is at the moment of elections; the most obvious center of representation is the legislature. Through elections, democracies can achieve that peaceful change of administration which is the most difficult of problems for dictatorship. Through legislatures, the public is kept informed of proposals for policy and lawmaking and hears them thrashed out in the battle of conflicting points of view. Moreover, through investigations—either by legislative committees as in the United States, or by the more flexible method of the parliamentary question—the executive may be kept under supervision even on points of administrative detail.

To say this, however, is not to answer a long series of questions, some of them substantive and some technical, but all revolving around these issues: How can representatives be kept responsible both to their own constituents and to the interests of the whole electorate? Whom should representatives represent, and how should they perform this function? And how should elections be conducted and on what electoral basis?

To be more specific: Should elections be held in single-member districts where the decision is always clear, or in multimember constituencies where the results, through proportional distribution of seats, more nearly reflect the popular vote? Part of the advantage of voting in single-member districts is that the contest is understandable and often dramatic, as in any race where only one person can win. Moreover, in this kind of voting there is no question but that the elected representative is directly responsible to a particular constituency as well as to the whole country in general. In addition, and very important, there is the fact that under this system powerful parties tend, at least in Anglo-Saxon countries, to win so high a proportion of the seats in the legislature that they easily fill the competitive roles of government and opposition. This makes for effective government, since the party in power has the votes to carry out its program; at the same time, the opposition becomes responsible for the clear presentation of alternative policies and for unremitting efforts to keep the government sensitive to its responsibilities.

The problem of single-member constituencies is that the minority stands in danger of being disenfranchised. Beyond the apparent injustice that up to 49 per cent of those who exercise their franchise may not have their voices count in the final selection of the representatives, the presence of third-party candidates, not so rare these days in either Great Britain or Canada, may split the vote so that the representative is chosen by as little as 34 per cent of the electors. Should there, therefore, be multi-member districts and a system of proportional representation, so that minorities will be represented more in proportion to their strength throughout the country? Proportional representation may mean voting for a list of party nominees from which the top names are selected in accordance with the number of votes the party secures; or using the single transferable vote, in which the elector ranges his candidates in order of preference and has his second choice counted if his first choice has either been elected already by other people's votes or has no chance of being so; or be combined with a final contest between two candidates selected through a "run-off" preliminary contest, as was used during the Third French Republic; or some other procedure. Regardless of details, the results of this system may seem to be fairer than those of contests in single-member constituencies. If Great Britain, for example, used proportional representation, the Liberal Party would have many more members in Parliament, for its proportion of the total vote is always much higher than its proportion of MP's.

But this system also may give rise to several problems. The elections under proportional representation are not so easy to follow as the other type; moreover, it is much more difficult to determine that highly important fact in a democratic system: to whom is the representative responsible? Since proportional representation also tends to maximize the voting power of small, closely knit minorities, it tends to split the legislature into so many parties that effective government becomes difficult, if not impossible.

Australia now uses proportional representation for electing the ten senators from each of its six states; Ireland, Israel, and a number of other smaller states have adopted one or another form of proportional representation. Most, if not all the large modern countries, however, seem to feel that the liabilities of PR (as proportional representation is commonly called) outweigh its advantages for choosing the members of the body which is the seat of political power: the lower house.

Some countries which do adhere to the system of proportionality (or, like West Germany, to something close to it) have tried to eliminate some of its shortcomings through special devices. In West Germany, a "5-per-cent clause" denies any representation in the legislature to parties which fail to poll a minimum of 5 per cent of the votes. This has successfully prevented the formation of splinter groups; perhaps even too successfully, because as a result all but two or three parties have tended to disappear from the political arena. Thus, as under the single-member district system, voters rally to only the largest groups, perhaps in part to "climb on the bandwagon." From the point of view of proportionality, this may be regrettable. It provides compensation, however, through the greater stability inherent in a system of a few large parties.

Few electoral systems, of course, make any attempt to satisfy exactly the concept that every vote should have equal weight. The British were among the last to allow double voting on the basis of special claims to representation: i.e., the university vote and the business-premises vote, both of which were abolished by the Labour government after World War II. But in most countries with single-member districts, there are fewer voters in rural than in urban constituencies, a situation justified by the argument (no longer so valid in these days of rapid communication) that scattered communities covering large areas should have this measure of compensation. Many American districts vary widely in size, while electoral provisions for state legislatures frequently provide great overrepresentation to the rural as compared to the urban population. It is legislative control of redistricting that has contributed to this situation in the United States; in Great Britain and South Africa, for example, this responsibility is vested in impartial commissions of judges. But the effort of South Africa to keep redistricting constantly abreast of changing population levels has provided its own problems, since the boundaries of constituencies have been redrawn after every five-year census, and thus between each major election. Such frequent changes (as has also been true of British redistricting since World War II) have tended to break down the sense of community within a constituency, which contributes so much to the reality of representation. On the other hand, where redistricting lags behind, there is the opposite and perhaps even greater evil of districts becoming drastically unequal as the result of population shifts.

Even with their extraordinarily frequent redistricting, the South African election returns do not follow the popular vote with any degree of exactitude. The Nationalist Party had not yet polled 50 per cent of the votes, but in 1958 it won 103 out of 156 seats in the House of Assembly. This discrepancy is partly the result of overweighting the rural vote, but it results more directly from a phenomenon also easily observable in British elections: the fact that the major opposition party (in South Africa the United Party, and in Great Britain the Labour Party) piles up such huge majorities in urban centers that it "wastes" many of its votes.

What seems evident from this brief survey is that there is no electoral system which exactly reflects popular views and divisions. This in itself is not necessarily a cause for concern. What is important is to secure a rough approximation of popular sentiment through means which are accepted by the public as legitimate. Thus, democratic states do not need to worry about attempting to provide any exact mathematical reflection of the electorate—an attempt doomed to failure before it begins—nearly so much as about obvious subterfuges to secure the advantage of particular groups (such as gerrymandering the boundaries of constituencies), since this undercuts the sense of legitimacy which makes the public trust electoral results.

Even when, as in France under the Fourth Republic, it was the center parties upholding constitutional government which devised electoral rules to their own advantage, they were threatening the system they hoped to save. This danger has also not been absent from postwar Germany and Italy, since the method of election, not being specified in their Constitutions, could be devised anew by parliament for each election. Election systems have therefore tended to depend on the calculations of parties or majorities as to which rules would serve them best, and thus have tended to become the football of party politics. Since powerful groups are tempted to abuse their power to disenfranchise small ones, such tactics inevitably help alienate parts of the electorate. Momentarily, the result might be to the advantage of stable government. But since the process of election is designed to provide representation with the aura of legitimacy, any drastic attempt to distort electoral provisions to the advantage of any group cannot but imperil the faith of the electorate in the democratic system as such.

In the new states of Africa, universal franchise is looked on, not surprisingly, as the key to political power. Where white minorities have long held control, as in South Africa and in Southern Rhodesia, the vote is the means of maintaining or securing power (as, indeed, it still is in parts of the South in the United States). The old conflict between education and economic standing, on the one side, and numbers, on the other, which was waged in earlier days in Western industrializing countries, now permeates the multiracial states, and in a more virulent form. No one can doubt that ultimately numbers will secure the influence in Africa they have elsewhere—the political equalitarianism of the democratic creed is too widely accepted elsewhere to be denied indefinitely there—but this is only the first step. The franchise can put people into power. It is far more difficult to ensure their continuing awareness of and responsiveness to the public will. This is particularly true in Asian and African countries which as yet have had little democratic experience, though at least some of them have shown us, as in India or Nigeria, that illiteracy is no bar to selecting their representatives, and particularly their leaders, shrewdly. Yet not only in the new countries, but also in the older democratic states the issue remains: how to maintain a genuine link between representatives and those who put them into office.

There is, in fact, no real sense in which one man elected by universal suffrage can be said to represent the interests and wishes of all the voters in his constituency, or even the majority of them. The best that he can do, whether he is in the British House of Commons, the American Congress, or the Nigerian or Indian legislature, is to be aware of the most deeply felt preferences of his constituents, to be responsive to the views of important individuals, and to keep in mind the interests of the most important pressure groups operating in his constituency, if indeed they can be reconciled. But still more important are the demands of his party, the activities of its leaders, and his own sense of responsibility for viewing issues in the light of public interest rather than the more narrowly conceived advantages of particular groups or places.

In this framework, what distinguishes democratic government is not that it is representative but that it is responsible. The highest records of voting have been those in the Soviet Union, Fascist Italy, and Hitler Germany; but since there is only one slate of candidates, the effect is merely, and inevitably, to endorse the existing regime and in no sense to check its use of power. Though democratic states naturally encourage wide use of the franchise (some, like Australia and Belgium, make voting compulsory under penalty of a fine), the significance of an election is not how many people vote, but that this process makes it possible to put a government into or out of office without violence and thereby keep it responsible to the electorate.

POLITICAL PARTIES

Political parties are the indispensable links between the people and the representative machinery of government. Their role is most obvious when an election is in prospect, but, in fact, they need to be continually operative if a democratic system is to work effectively. It is political parties that organize the vastly diversified public by nominating candidates for office and by popularizing the ideas around which governmental programs are built. They are the vehicles through which individuals and groups work to secure political power and, if successful, to exercise that power. What differentiates political parties from interest or pressure groups is the breadth and variety of their followings and the orientation of their programs toward issues of concern to the whole country. Because awakening interest in these broader questions is a more difficult task than stimulating interest in matters which obviously affect the business or family of an individual, parties must make people politically conscious, i.e., aware of their role as citizens. This role is not discharged simply at the moment of voting but must be a continuous one if government is to be kept responsive to public interests. Thus, political parties are responsible for maintaining a continuous connection between the public and those who represent it either in the government or in the opposition.

CONTRAST BETWEEN DEMOCRATIC AND DICTATORIAL PARTIES

Dictatorships also find the political party an indispensable instrument, but they use it in a very different way than do democracies. Where democratic political parties consciously emphasize diversity and mutual criticism, the political party in the Communist or Fascist dictatorship is the body of the faithful who are dedicated to maintaining the one truth which their leaders avow. Whereas, apart from their elected members, democratic political parties are informal, nongovernmental organizations (though particularly in the United States their activities must be carried on within a network of governmental regulations), the dictatorial political party permeates every governmental as well as nongovernmental activity and is virtually indistinguishable, except in name, from the administration which it dominates. Where democratic systems maximize opportunities for criticism and protect individual rights to free speech, dictatorial systems operate on the principle of "democratic centralism," i.e., that comments may be offered only in the early stages of a proposal, but once the leaders have made their decision everyone must accept it. Where democracies anticipate an alternation of leaders and provide the public with a choice of candidates for office, dictatorial leaders are self-selected through a power struggle within the party machinery itself. Where democracies use the fervor and slogans of an electoral campaign to publicize the differences between party programs, the party in a dictatorial state carries on continual propaganda campaigns in support of the government's objectives and is the chief means by which conformity is maintained throughout the society.

It is thus confusing and, in a sense, inappropriate to use the term "political party" not only for the competing political associations in democratic states but also for that group which has the full monopoly of political as well as of all other powers in a dictatorial totalitarian state. A prime characteristic of political parties as they have evolved in democratic countries is that they are voluntary groupings which acquire their cohesion from perceived and accepted purposes. Democratic political parties also socially integrate the people within their ranks by giving them a common objective and a common organization. But the political party in such states is a vehicle to be used by its members, not a master to give them orders. In totalitarian states, in contrast, the political party is the chief means of control throughout the state, and thus its membership is carefully sifted to ensure conformity to the overriding purpose of the small governing group. To a certain degree the political party serves the purpose of expressing the sentiments of its members, but only to the degree that is useful for the purposes of the regime. In no case does it act to restrain the exercise of power. As the Nazis used to put it: in democracies authority comes from below and responsibility from above; in dictatorships authority comes from above and responsibility from below.

THE TOTALITARIAN PARTY IN A DEMOCRATIC STATE

The fundamental differences between democratic- and totalitarian-minded parties raise particular problems when one of the latter is operating within a democratic state. At the beginning of the century, Lenin taught his Bolsheviks the secret of successful subversion: to be a highly organized, highly disciplined group giving unquestioned obedience to its leaders in tactics, in their interpretation of Marxist dogma, and in their objective of radically reorganizing society. Hitler used much the same techniques in building his Nazi party into an instrument capable of taking over power from the Weimar Republic. Thus, fascist and Communist parties are always suspected of seeking to overthrow the legitimate government of the country within which they work, and replacing it, if necessary by force, with their own control—either in their own interests or, in the case of a Communist Party, the interests of a leading Communist-controlled country: the Soviet Union or China.

Totalitarian-minded parties are most effective in seizing control within states whose machinery of government is weak and indecisive and whose population has little sense of common unity. But even without the hope of replacing the legitimate government with their own, totalitarian-minded parties can do much to disturb the smooth functioning of the state. In postwar France, the Communists regularly polled 25 to 30 per cent of the vote in elections and, at least until the Fifth French Republic, placed a large number of their representatives in Parliament. In Italy, much the same has happened. This process has two debilitating effects on democratic operations: It withdraws a large number of voters from support of democratically inclined parties and forces them to compete within the restricted milieu of perhaps 70 per cent of the politically conscious public; and it places a strong group of deputies in a position where they can constantly harass the administration and thus divert it from its primary job of providing effective, responsible government.

The Communist vote in France and Italy does not reflect a comparable degree of mass support. In each case, there is a relatively small, highly organized group of militants who are dedicated to Marxism-Leninism, and a much larger number of people whose grievances these militants exploit by playing on the strains caused by rising costs of living, or unattractive conditions in mining, or shipping, or the civil service. As long as there is no chance of their securing political power, Communist Parties do not seem capable of securing majority support. This is part of the reason why Communists joined in French Popular Front governments, as under Léon Blum in the mid-thirties, and after World War II, but in each case the ultimate awareness of their democratically minded partners that the Communists were seeking their own advantage rather than that of the whole country led to their ejection.

Similar situations have developed in regard to the Communist Party in India. As the only organized group endorsing the Indian war effort (which it did because the Soviet Union was involved), the Communist Party had special opportunities to develop during World War II. Shortly thereafter, and for the first two years of India's independence, the Communists were revolutionary in aims and actions. Dealt with firmly by Pandit Nehru's government, the Communist Party then announced that it accepted the democratic framework and would secure its purposes through the peaceful winning of elections. Although the Congress Party has maintained its predominant position in India, as we have noted, the Communists now form the second largest party in Parliament, though they constitute only a small proportion of its total membership. Still more disturbing was their electoral success in Kerala, one of the most highly literate but economically depressed of Indian states. After two years of Communist administration, anti-Communist groups used passive-resistance techniques against the Communist regime in Kerala, until ultimately enough disorder occurred so that the national government exercised its constitutional right to take over the state administration. New elections were held under a somewhat revised electoral system which gave non-Communist parties a majority in the legislature, although the Communists retained a majority of the votes. Perhaps the most significant fact in the situation was the rapid increase in the mass support of the Communist Party during the period it was in office. This fact provides a serious warning of what might happen in India if the Congress Party should disintegrate—a warning important for any democratic state with a strongly entrenched Communist Party.

Because of the fear of Communist infiltration, some states, in particular South Africa and West Germany, as we have seen, have outlawed their Communist Parties. But this tactic runs the danger either of forcing the organization underground, where it may be still more dangerous or, as in South Africa, of using broadly phrased anti-Communist legislation to suppress legitimate efforts to change discriminatory practices. It is far more constructive to attack those conditions and grievances which the Communist Party can exploit, and to develop the national consensus and its reflection in mass popular parties which provide the best insurance against the rise of totalitarian-minded groups. At this point, therefore, it is important to consider the development of the mass party in democratic states.

THE RISE OF THE MASS PARTY

Although political parties are now recognized as the dynamic of the democratic political process and the chief means whereby popular control can be exercised, this has not always been the case. When organized political parties first arose in Great Britain and on the Continent, they were aristocratic cliques or factions seeking to protect the interests of their particular group against monarchical demands, although, especially in Britain, some of their members had a strong sense of public responsibility. With the rise of the bourgeoisie came what Max Weber calls "parties of notables," informal associations built around those persons who actually held parliamentary seats. This stage of party development was characteristic of British parties after the Parliamentary Reform of 1832, of the political groups in the German Parliament of 1848, of parties in pre-Fascist Italy, and among the center and rightist groups under the French Third Republic. There is also a parallel in the efforts of the Federalists in the early days of American independence to preserve the monopoly of political office by persons of property and position.

But this stage of party development has virtually ceased to exist. In its place is the mass party, as evident in the United States and Great Britain as it is in India or Mexico. The mass party is the natural outcome of universal suffrage and of the need to appeal broadly to different groups in the community. In contrast to the earlier party of notables, the mass party not only attempts to appeal to all groups in the community, but also tends to be highly organized on a national level (at least at election time), with increasing power resting in the hands of party functionaries. At the same time, it is the mass party's representatives in parliament who are ultimately responsible for policies, and they rarely abdicate this responsibility to the professional party organization which did so much to put them into office.

Political parties in the older democracies, and especially the older, more conservative parties, reached the stage of mass appeal and professional country-wide organization only by degrees. In the United States, parties are still organized largely at the state level and become national organizations only at four-year intervals. In Germany, the "bourgeois" parties, such as the present Christian Democratic Party, have still not attained the degree of cohesion which has long been characteristic of the Social Democrats, as can be seen from the much lower percentage of the Christian Democrats' formal membership, not to mention the greater interest in party affairs taken by the average member of the SPD. Even in Great Britain, the Conservative Party only slowly adopted the high degree of organization it possesses today, and then largely to counter the impact of Labour, whose popular appeal and disciplined cohesion were its strongest weapons against the entrenched economic strength of the two older British parties. In both Australia and New Zealand, the more conservative parties—the Liberal Party in Australia and the National Party in New Zealand—were even slower to develop a high degree of organization or a popular mass appeal, doing so only as late as the elections of 1949, at which time they both ousted Labour administrations from office. In contrast, neither the Liberal nor the Conservative Party in Canada is as yet highly organized, except at election time. In that country as in the United States, political parties tend to be great holding companies, incorporating conflicting interests and maintaining their cohesion through the imprint of characteristic attitudes—the Canadian Liberals and the American Democrats being innovators and social-minded, whereas the concern of Canadian Conservatives and American Republicans is directed toward the balanced budget—as well as through the struggle for political power. Under these circumstances, there is less need to develop highly organized national structures such as are characteristic of present-day British parties or socialist parties on the Continent.

A distinction can be made, in fact, between what is called a party of individual representation and a party of social integration. The former is concerned only with political functions, as is still largely true in Canada and the United States, and even with these on a limited scale. Although the appeal is directed at the whole community, it is generally made only at election time. Moreover, the representative, once chosen, feels free to make his own judgments on issues, to the detriment of party solidarity —a particular characteristic of Southern Democrats in the United States, but by no means restricted to them. The party of social integration, on the other hand, demands much more of its members in terms of financial support, of continuous concern with issues, and of a coordinated view of life. Its representatives are under stricter party discipline. Socialist parties are those which most obviously fit this latter definition, but as government assumes more responsibilities for economic and social life, there is a natural trend toward turning any party of representation into one of social integration. As long as it neither aims at the total integration of dictatorships nor operates in so exclusivist a fashion as to imperil the basic consensus on which all stable democratic societies must rest, this process does not threaten but complements the mass democracy of the twentieth century.

This danger of imperiling basic consensus is illustrated, however, by one of the most distinctive of modern mass parties, the Nationalist Party in South Africa. Even in the nineteenth century, the Afrikaner people were organizing themselves into groups with suggestive names like *Het Volk* (the people). Within two years of the coming into being of the South African Parliament in 1910, the first

Afrikaner Nationalist Party was formed. When the contemporary Nationalist Party acquired sole governing power in the Union for the first time in 1948, it had become as completely the political representative of the great mass of the Afrikaner people as the Dutch Reformed Church was their religious vehicle. Moreover, the Nationalists have developed a highly organized party machinery which uses professionals to direct the constant activities of a large body of volunteer workers. Thus the strength of the party rests on two virtually unassailable pillars: a high degree of organization; and a fervent sense of separate identity of the Afrikaner people, which can be constantly reinforced by appeals to their genuine fear of cultural as well as physical submergence by the numerically dominant non-whites.

The Nationalists represent an unusually close identification of a political party with a particular racial group. So close an identification, whether with a particular racial or social group, may well mean, as we shall see later, that the representative aspect of a political party outweighs the responsible aspect. In other words, a political party, like a political representative, has two functions: it must heed the wishes and interests of those who have put it into office as well as of the formal membership of its group, but it ought also to have regard for the interests of the whole country. For either political program or political leadership to be limited to the narrow interests of a single group may tend to split or to distort the character of the community if that party acquires political power.

TWO-PARTY VERSUS MULTIPARTY SYSTEMS

The sharp and fundamental distinction between political party systems, as we have seen, is between those in totalitarian and those in democratic countries. But there are also very considerable differences between characteristically two-party systems such as we find in Great Britain, the United States, Canada, Australia, New Zealand, and South Africa, and the multiparty systems of Continental Europe. Most of the traditional two-party systems also include one or more smaller parties, as Great Britain, for example, includes the Liberal Party; Canada, the Cooperative Commonwealth Federation (CCF) and the Social Credit Party; South Africa, the Liberal and, since 1959, the Progressive Parties, etc. But the essential contest is between two parties only. The third, or the third and fourth parties, may secure a limited number of seats, but not enough to become the official opposition. Thus the election takes on the characteristic of a contest between two major opposing forces; and the voter may cast his vote for a political group which is certain either to form the government or to become its constant critic.

In multiparty systems, however, the voter can never be sure whether the party for which he votes is going to form the central part of a governing coalition or not. The process of compromise which goes on within a given political party in the average two-party system (and particularly in one like the American or Canadian system, which finds business, labor, and farmers in both major parties) is transferred in a multiparty system to the floor of the assembly, or to the chambers where party leaders meet to hammer out the composition and program of a coalition government. This often enhances the authority of the assembly and the independence of the ordinary member of that body. Unless his party is a strongly disciplined one, like the French Communist or even the French Socialist Party, the member has a chance to exercise his own discretion about policies, and particularly about who should be the premier, in a way which is completely foreign to two-party systems. The penalty (and it is a big one) is that governments tend to rise and fall with dismaying regularity, as they did in both the Third and the postwar Fourth Republics in France. Moreover, it is difficult to secure continuity of policies except through the action of the administration, which is thereby enhanced in power.

It is common to say that what determines whether there is a two-party or multiparty system is the degree of unity of the particular community. Multiparty systems obviously reflect divisions within the community, divisions in social structure, economic interest, racial composition, or ideological preference. But that naturally disparate groups can be held together by a strong personality and the overriding importance of a few major issues has been proved by the experience of West Germany. Much the same task as Dr. Adenauer performed in West Germany was carried out successfully by Pandit Nehru in India during its transition to a linguistic basis for federalism. But when cleavages go deep in a country and are felt intensely, only exceptional circumstances and leadership—like that of General Charles de Gaulle in France—are capable of bridging them. Moreover, unless new allegiances develop which are stronger than the divisive factors, multiparty divisions tend to take hold again and once more seriously to handicap effective government should that leadership be removed.

But two-party systems have their own problems. This is true especially where, as in Great Britain, Australia, and New Zealand, parties divide on a class basis, or where, as in Canada and South Africa, there are racial divisions to be bridged. Before 1924, some political observers even believed that Labour would never be able to achieve office in Great Britain without a violent reaction, since they felt that the propertied groups in the community would feel too threatened by its objectives to allow such a program to be imposed peacefully. That this did not happen reflects a major degree of agreement on fundamentals between the Labour Party and the other parties in Great Britain and New Zealand as well as in Australia (where Labour achieved national office as early as 1908). It also reflects the fact that the programs introduced by Labour, when it came into office in those countries, corresponded to the social conscience or, in the latter two countries, to the equalitarian views, of the community at that particular moment.

This explains two phenomena: why Labour was able to carry through its program so quickly and without difficulty in all three of these countries, and why in each case the Labour Party tended to lose its momentum and appeal so soon after instituting its reforms. What seems obvious is that once a simple reformist program has been carried through by a labor party, it confronts the much more difficult issue of whether to introduce more than palliatives to curb the inequities and dislocations inherent in capitalism. It confronts the dilemma, in other words, of whether to be representative of its own particularism, or whether to be responsible to the basic ways of action of the whole community. If it drastically attacks the prevailing economic modes, it risks alienating its own right wing and even more the middle-class groups on which it depends for electoral success. If not, it alienates its own more radical members and loses its drive. Thereafter, paradoxically, its greatest appeal to the electorate may well be that it can do better administratively than its conservative opponents—who in the meantime have adopted the more attractive parts of labor's program. The end result in these cases is that the consensus of the community is strengthened, while effective government is maintained.

That it is possible for this process also to take place where racial rather than social and economic divisions are concerned is proved by the experience of Canada. In that country, with the exception of the split over conscription between English- and French-Canadians during World War I, the national-party system has never reflected racial divisions. The French-speaking minority is always represented within the governing party (in the long Liberal reign from 1935 to 1957, virtually all of Quebec's representatives were on the government side), and this ensures consideration of its distinctive point of view. The fact that the English- and French-speaking population work together in the same party, or parties, also aids mutual understanding and the building of consensus.

In South Africa, in contrast, the United Party, which then combined practically all the English-speaking population with a small percentage of Afrikaans-speaking South Africans under an Afrikaner leader, was dispossessed of political power in 1948 by the Nationalist Party with its exclusively Afrikaner membership and leadership. The result has been a noticeable sharpening of racial feeling between the two groups. Largely because all white people in the Union are conscious of their need to retain something of a common front against the non-whites, who outnumber them four to one, the division between Afrikaners and English-speaking people has not become dangerous. This experience suggests, however, that a political party composed of one racial (or any other exclusivist) group tends to accentuate divisions in a country, and thus either to lessen the nation's consensus or to result in an imposed new pattern of conformity. Thus, somewhat paradoxically, the two-party system, which is so often the reflection of a basic agreement on fundamentals, may also become a means of imposing the will of a parliamentary majority upon a reluctant minority.

PARTY FINANCING

With the rise of the mass party, the question of who pays for party work and party offices, party employees and, in particular, campaign and other election expenditures has become an ever more urgent one. At the time of party "notables," persons of independent means could still finance their own campaigns. While this fact, of course, favored wealth, it was so to speak self-contained wealth, and the successful candidate, on the whole, was not beholden to persons or groups which backed him financially in expectation of reward. Today, the financing of a mass party and its election campaign requires vast amounts of money, which, in principle, can be secured in two ways: by the ordinarily small contributions of party members and voters, or by the fewer but larger subsidies on the part of special-interest groups, such as business enterprises, agricultural organizations, and trade unions. In our days, and especially since the organization of nationwide campaigns (with, for example, their arrangements for television and radio appearances of candidates) has become a fine and expensive art, the questions of from whom and how a party secures its major support can be decisive not only for its subsequent attitudes and policies, but for its very success at the polls.

It is here that the functioning of the democratic process meets a vital test. If equality of opportunity in the political field is to have more than a mere formal meaning, it must imply at least some degree of equality in the means essential for political success. But this ideal is far from being realized in most democratic systems. It is well known that in the United States, the Republican Party is usually favored over the Democratic Party in regard to availability of campaign funds (in the 1956 election roughly by 2:1). The most striking recent example of such "inequality in financial opportunity" is perhaps that of West Germany, where industry has established so-called "promoters' associations," which assess the individual enterprises according to their payroll and distribute the levies among the government parties (with the chief portion, of course, going to the CDU). The Social Democrats, compelled to rely on membership fees and similar small contributions, have been able to spend only about one-fourth of the amount available to the CDU. In Great Britain, a system more effective in limiting campaign expenditures than that in the United States has prevented the extremes of these plutocratic abuses. In Canada, big business commonly contributes to both major parties, though a higher percentage is given to the one in power. But the problem is a serious one. Unless and until they solve it, democracies will continue to be exposed to charges that behind their egalitarian façade rich men or powerful interests are in control.

THE MASS PARTY IN THE NEWER STATES

While mass parties evolved slowly in the older democratic states, they have been a characteristic of the newer states from the beginning. Where a nationalistic movement is struggling to bring a country to independence, its natural focus is in a mass party which unites virtually all elements in the country in a common demand for transfer of power. As independence comes close or is achieved, strains may develop, however, which split the mass party into communal or tribally oriented groups. In British India, for example, the Moslem League refused to work with the Congress Party with its largely Hindu support and secular philosophy, and the ultimate result was that the subcontinent had to be partitioned between Pakistan and India.

In the Republic of India, the Congress Party has managed to maintain its dominant position despite challenges from both the socialist parties on the left and the communal parties on the right, but largely because of the personal magnetism of Pandit Nehru rather than because of its own vigor. In Pakistan, the Moslem League split badly after losing its best leaders through death or assassination, and the country is now under army rule.

In the Gold Coast (subsequently Ghana), middle-class and tribally oriented groups combined against the standard-bearer of nationalism, Kwame Nkrumah's Convention Peoples Party (commonly known as the CPP), in the years immediately preceding independence. In an effort to satisfy them, the British insisted that Ghana should establish regional assemblies to share power with the national legislature, but these were voted out of existence almost as soon as they came into being; moreover, the opposition has steadily diminished in strength, due partly to governmental arbitrariness, partly to its own policy and tactical mistakes, and partly to the difficulty of retaining support without being able to provide the kind of benefits which government can bestow. Rapid and impressive development plans have done much to unify Ghana but also further to strengthen Nkrumah's government, and it seems unlikely that the opposition will be able in the foreseeable future to challenge its power.

Is there then no middle way between a dominant mass party in newly developing states and anarchy threatening to lead to army or dictatorial rule? Possibly not. The problem of emerging Asian and African states still is more social than political: It is the need to build a strong enough sense of unity in the country so that criticism and diversity do not appear to be treason. Wherever there is a serious split in the nationalist movement prior to independence, the group which stands in opposition is almost inevitably labeled treasonable. If this split persists after independence, either force or a long period of stability are needed to heal it. The kind of divisions which are welcomed in well-established democracies may shatter the fragile chances of national unity in tribally oriented societies.

ONE-PARTY DEMOCRACY

In Tanganyika, most promising of the multiracial states (its small percentage of white persons and the somewhat larger Asian component support the African nationalist movement), Julius Nyerere, founder and leader of the Tanganyika African National Union, which is progressively taking over political responsibilities as the country moves steadily toward independence, speaks eloquently of "one-party democracy." Nyerere's view is that everyone must combine within the mass party which is leading the country to self-rule and that this same mass party will inevitably conduct the government after independence has been won. He refuses to acknowledge the right to criticism of anyone not within this movement. At the same time, he asserts that anyone who does dedicate himself to the progress of independence is justified in criticizing the actions of the governing group and even in establishing an alternative political party if the nationalist standard-bearer should fail in its tasks of building social solidarity and stimulating economic growth. The difference between this contention and developments in Ghana is that in Tanganyika opposition must arise from *within* the nationalistic group to be recognized as legitimate.

Is this democracy? We have been accustomed to say that one-party rule and dictatorship were virtually synonymous. But even in the early days of the United States, there was only one party, the Federalists, until Jefferson stimulated the rise of what was little more than a personal political movement. When the Federalist Party collapsed, the country was left for some time without an organized alternative to Jefferson's Republican Party. Yet in the long run, of course, the American two-party system emerged. While it is natural for the older Western democracies to look for two-party systems and ultimate alternation of office in the new countries, these require experience, a substantial pool of talent, and a fairly firm social structure. It has developed, and may well last, in Nigeria, where the very diversity of the three regions encourages such a process. But for most of the new countries, the touchstone of democracy will be the right to express open criticism and the maintenance of the rule of law. If these two essentials exist, the future may well see the evolution of what we consider the more orthodox structure of democratic government.

What we have called "one-party democracy" differs basically, it must be emphasized, from the one-party totalitarianism of the Soviet Union itself or other Communist-controlled countries. To have only one party in the first instance is not a dogma but an expedient. The objective is to mobilize the people voluntarily to work for the vastly important objective of national development.

In this sense, "one-party democracy" parallels the unity most Western democratic states established while they were fighting what President Franklin D. Roosevelt called "the war of survival"—World War II. In contrast, the "peoples' democracies" accept one-party rule as permanent, stamp out opposition, and regard the party as the agent to secure conformism. Thus, despite occasional relaxations, they are far closer to Soviet totalitarianism than to Nyerere's "one-party demcracy."

The possibilities of criticism within the one-party democracy provide in themselves a type of opposition which should not be underestimated. The mass parties in the newly developing countries are far from monolithic. It is far more difficult to identify and classify the kind of opposition which operates, for example, within Félix Houphouet-Boigny's RDA (*Rassemblement Démocratique Africain*), which holds all the seats in the Ivory Coast, than it would be if the opposition were organized as a separate party—but its existence has been abundantly evidenced by changing policies. In other words, something very close to the interplay of government and opposition in mature democracies may take place within the one party of the new states, but only, of course, if opportunities for criticism are not stifled.

ARMY RULE

In a striking number of cases, new parliamentary democracies which failed to work efficiently have come under army rule. In the Sudan, in Pakistan, in Burma, in Egypt, in Iraq, and once again in Turkey, military leaders have been or are running the civilian machinery of government. In part, these situations have been the result of internal or external threats, in particular by Communists

Channels of Political Action

or by Nasser, but more especially they arose out of parliamentary crises and weaknesses. Western democracies look with disquiet at the establishment of military dictatorships, and rightly so, though the examples of General Eisenhower and, to a lesser extent, General de Gaulle prove that generals can be good democrats. In the new countries, however, the army sometimes possesses more liberally minded and well-trained people than are found among the politicians. (This was much less true in Latin America in the past than it now is in Asia.) General Ne Win assumed leadership in Burma in October, 1958, as the result of an agreement between feuding, popularly elected leaders. General Mohammed Ayub Khan, who also took over in 1958, has reformed the administration in Pakistan and is moving gradually toward a more responsible regime. In Turkey, the overthrow of the Menderes government by army leaders in the late spring of 1960 ended a regime which had grown increasingly illiberal and opened the way to possible reform. In none of these cases can army rule be looked on as an unmitigated blessing, the more so because of the danger that subsequent coups, like the one in which Colonel Nasser replaced General Naguib in Egypt or those which failed to dislodge General Ibrahim Abboud in the Sudan in 1959, may lead either to expansionism or to bloodshed. Nonetheless, it is not beyond the bounds of possibility that army rule may provide useful discipline and a marked improvement in integrity within new countries and thereby improve the chances of democratic regimes when, as has happened in Burma, they are established once more.

Much depends, of course, on the program of the army leader who comes into power. There is a similarity between the forms of local representation adopted in Egypt and in Pakistan under Nasser and Ayub Khan respectively, yet there is a vast difference in the methods they use in attempting to shape their respective societies. As far as institutions are concerned, both have established directly elected village and town councils as the lowest level of representation, arguing with some justification that illiterate peasants can choose better from among those they know personally than between rival parties. Ayub Khan has divided West and East Pakistan into 40,000 constituencies, each with an average population of 1,000; each constituency elects one representative by universal suffrage. Ten rural constituencies form a Union Council, and Town Committees are similarly established. The chairmen of these councils form the Thana Council, which has duties and responsibilities within the area of a police station. Ultimately, this system is intended to move upward. Nasser's National Union is already the top of a pyramid in which each successive level of territorial councils is selected by the personnel of those in the next lower level of councils.

This attempt to substitute consensus in a representative system for party government is said to avoid unnatural divisions and to reflect the so-called traditional "village democracy" of which Asian and African leaders sometimes boast. But while Ayub Khan is concentrating on land reform and tackling local problems, Nasser has embarked on a radical reorganization of the economy, using nationalization as a major instrument. Under these latter circumstances, the establishment of a nonparty representative system can all too easily be molded into an instrument to enforce uniformity of response to centrally and possibly arbitrarily formulated policies. In the case of Pakistan, the village-oriented social and economic program on which Ayub Khan has embarked has a much more direct relationship to the local councils which form the current basis of representation than is the case with the radical program now operating in Egypt.

It is open to question, however, whether in the long run any representative system based on the hypothesis that decisions must be the result of general consensus or agreement can avoid the danger of crushing opportunities for the expression of independent thinking. "Village democracy" arose out of circumstances providing limited alternatives or even an absence of alternatives. It reflects narrow horizons, perhaps bounded by the physical limits of the village itself. As the village becomes part of a much larger entity with a wide range of alternatives and is affected by swift-moving social and economic change, the strain on the traditional consensus becomes great. It is true that the conventional approval of consensus as the means of reaching decisions may survive long after the circumstances have ended which produced its expectation. Moreover, the longing for either a "right answer" intuitively perceived or for the broadest common denominator of agreement is found in mature societies as well as in those which have recently been formed out of what were more or less isolated village or rural entities. But the challenge involved in the presentation of alternatives may well imply the existence, or even creation, of a greater degree of basic consensus than does the uniformity of view resulting from an overemphasis on the value of harmony and a consequent blurring of the edges of genuine controversy. There is an arithmetical, if not a geometrical, relationship between the number of possible alternatives of action and the speed of social and economic change. The opportunity to argue out these alternatives, at least in the interest of understandability and of a check on possible arbitrariness, may well produce a more solidly knit community than institutions which are directed toward glossing over such differences of view.

It is not only under army rule that such issues arise. The one-party democracies of which we have spoken are also eager to enjoy a consensus in regard to their policies. Since popular support is necessarily one of the criteria by which we judge the degree of democracy of such regimes, it is particularly important to be alert to the degree to which that support is secured through techniques which muffle opposition, or genuinely arises as the result of the interaction of alternatives.

Army rule in areas other than the United Arab Republic and Pakistan has had still more widely varied effects. In Burma, it provided a successful transition to more stable parliamentary rule. In the Sudan, in contrast, there is little evidence that army rule has improved what was admittedly an unstable situation under the regime of parties. A series of army coups in the first months of the military regime resulted in broadening the base of authority, but ultimately it led to bloodshed. In Iraq, army rule has provided more stability than in the Sudan but less than in any of the other countries of which we have been speaking. Thus it is evident that the character of the army leadership and, perhaps still more important, the existing social structure determine the impact of army rule. Both Ayub Khan and Nasser have seen the need to approach the basic problems of underdeveloped societies at the local level, but the impetuousness and violence of change in contemporary Egypt may nullify the efforts to make local communities a source of political influence and thus keep army rule a revolutionary force.

The experience of Turkey follows none of these patterns. Turkey was transformed from a traditionalist

Islamic state to a secular republic and acquired stability, economic growth, and a secure international position under the authoritarian rule of its great leader, Kemal Pasha, better known as Atatürk. In 1945, the country was precipitously introduced by President Inönü to a multi-party Western-style parliamentary system with popular elections. As a result of free elections, the initial opposition acquired political power in 1950. But on May 27, 1960, the ten-year-old Menderes regime—which, for all its known corruptness, had widespread popular support, particularly among the peasants who had always resisted the Atatürk reforms—was overthrown by an army group which aimed at improving standards of morality and conditions of life. This group, somewhat modified in composition, retained power far beyond its original intention, since the leaders of opinion throughout the country divide between the Western-minded liberals who want reform rather than a changed system and those who question whether parliamentary government on the Western model can meet the urgent needs of a country with a 70 per cent illiteracy rate, a 3 per cent annual birth rate, and severe economic and social problems.

This remains a basic question for all underdeveloped countries. It is easy to answer it with either the view that authoritarianism is essential to maintain stability and to demand the sacrifices for development, or with its opposite: i.e., that parliamentary institutions provide the framework within which leadership can be combined with public airing of issues and restraint on arbitrary action. Neither view is necessarily valid for particular situations. It is important to recognize that the operation of parliamentary institutions in such a way as to provide effective and yet responsible government requires a considerable degree of experience and of restraint. Turkey itself may have been too precipitous in introducing this political system. The Belgians obviously gave such institutions little or no chance of success in the Congo by bestowing them only a few weeks before the territory achieved independence on June 30, 1960. Yet among the former British and former French territories of West Africa, some—like Nigeria, Ghana, Senegal, and the Ivory Coast—have not been unsuccessful in handling parliamentary institutions. The latter provide legitimacy and a known method of succession in a way which authoritarian regimes cannot duplicate. At their best, they also provide for the ventilation of issues so that feelings are not bottled up until they reach the explosion point.

What the experience of army rule and one-party democracies may indicate is that the urge to express opposing views, and the corrective balance wheel to authoritarianism of such outlets, may be found in many more places than traditional political analysis has suggested. Within a democratic one-party system, the opposition may make itself felt through trade unions or youth or women's groups; it may be provided by the army acting in a nonpolitical but somewhat censorlike role; or by the civil service acting in the same nonpartisan fashion and allowed by the ruling politicians to do so. As long as this is the case, the stifling effects of authoritarianism are lessened, the opportunities for social growth enhanced, and cohesion and stability combined with criticism. In comparison with this somewhat sensitive balance, unresponsive dictatorship—whether veiled in parliamentary forms or those built on a system of village councils, or exercised openly to the accompaniment of inflammatory nationalist propaganda—tends to an enforced uniformity within which opposition can express itself only through violence.

LEGISLATURES

The end result of the activity of political parties is to place their candidates in the legislature. In some countries, both the lower and upper houses are popularly elected and thus serve to fulfill the representational function. In the United States, not only the House of Representatives and the Senate, but also the President have the basis of direct popular support. In Australia, another federal country, the Senate is also popularly elected. But in France and South Africa, for example, the second chamber is selected by an indirect method, which tends to make it both more conservative than the lower chamber and also much weaker. In Great Britain, of course, the second chamber rests on hereditary succession; in Canada, senators are appointed. In these two countries, the second chamber tends to sink into the background and to be useful largely as a place for consideration of issues which the popularly elected chamber does not have time adequately to explore.

Where, as in the presidential-congressional system of the United States, direct election underpins the power and prestige of both legislative chambers and of the chief executive as well, there is a natural basis for the system of checks and balances which can operate despite the links among all three created by political parties. But in a parliamentary system, where the executive is not separate from the legislature, there is an almost irresistible tendency toward the dominance of either the cabinet or the lower chamber, even if both legislative bodies are elective. Few chambers were so buttressed in power as the French National Assembly under the Fourth Republic; under the Fifth Republic it has become a mere shadow of its former self as the Cabinet and President have become dominant. The British House of Commons occupies a position midway between the French National Assembly of the Fourth and Fifth Republics—a body of distinction but under the control of the Cabinet.

The person who seeks for "representative" government in the sense of a parliamentary body which conducts all the affairs of state, originating the laws and directing their administration, is bound in any case to be disappointed: but the fault lies in his expectations rather than in a weakness of democratic machinery. Representative government, in this sense, could not exist under even the best of circumstances. To expect any large and varied group of average inexpert representatives to frame the laws of a complex society and to coordinate all the government's far-flung activities is to impose a burden which no representative assembly was intended to bear.

What a well-organized assembly can do—and do well—is to analyze, criticize, and judge the policies and proposals of the government; to voice the desires and anxieties of the mass of the citizens; to protect their liberties against any abuse of power by the government; to educate public opinion through its debates; and to supervise the way in which legislation is administered. In some ways, the legislature is particularly suited to these tasks. If its members lack the expert knowledge necessary to frame technical legislation, they possess a different kind of knowledge which the experts themselves are not likely to have: the legislators, taken in the mass, represent a range of experience in terms of class and geographical origin and in intimate knowledge of their constituents which makes them exceptionally good judges of public opinion and of the acceptability and workability of laws.

In the Soviet Union, as one would expect, the aim is different; the Supreme Soviet is, in practice, expected to perform only a few of these functions. Great care is taken to make that body as representative as possible in a vocational and a national sense; but the purpose is not to permit these representatives to oversee and control the government, but rather to permit the government to educate them (and through them the people) in its purposes and policies. Thus there is no criticism of the government's official policies, and what criticism there is of administration stops short of the leaders of the Communist Party and, presumably, is permitted only with their approval. The same applies to Soviet satellites, such as the People's Chamber of the German Democratic Republic.

When one turns to the Western democracies, it is evident that both the British Parliament and the French National Assembly under the Fourth Republic performed certain (though not the same) functions admirably. As protector of individual liberties against any abuse of governmental power, the House of Commons is unexcelled. As educator of the public on important issues, its well-organized debates are remarkably effective. As critic of proposed legislation, the opposition, at its best, is highly effective. The chief criticisms to which Parliament is subjected concern its lack of expertness (which detracts both from the cogency of its legislative criticism and from its ability to supervise the increasingly complex activities of the civil service), the rigor of party discipline (which allegedly destroys the independence and initiative of the private member), the failure to reflect with exactness the strength and varieties of political opinion in Great Britain, and subserviency to the Cabinet.

In postwar France of the Fourth Republic, in contrast, the National Assembly more accurately reflected the diversity of opinion and the popular vote, and the system of specialized committees provided members with greater knowledge and rendered them more fit to cope with the technicalities of modern legislation and administration. Although there were complaints of excessive discipline among some of the parties of the left, the deputies in the center and on the right enjoyed a large degree of independence. And, unlike the British Parliament, in normal times the French National Assembly demonstrates its control over the Cabinet by rejecting or making serious modifications in its proposals. In spite of these merits, however, few people would cite the Fourth Republic's National Assembly as a model of what a democratic legislative body ought to be. The inability of the different party groups to agree upon an effective legislative program and to support a stable government, the violent and undisciplined debate and the uncompromising hostility between different political interests, the eagerness of certain partisans on the extreme left and the extreme right to discredit parliamentary democracy by making effective action impossible, all helped to give currency to the popular picture of the legislature as a forum of bickering, irresponsible, special interests. This tended to make men readier to follow a leader who promised political stability and the placing of national above party interests, and thus paved the way for De Gaulle's Fifth Republic.

Nor does the German Parliament, whether under the Weimar or the present Bonn Republic, present a much more reassuring picture. Traditionally, the German executive had possessed more independence from parliament and parties than had the French executive, with the result that in Germany, Parliament's control of the executive was often ineffectual. The ensuing conflicts between popular forces and an authoritarian-minded governing elite discredited democratic procedures and representative institutions time and again, thereby opening the way for the executive to assume uncontrolled power.

Today, while it would be exaggerated to suggest that the executive is unrestricted politically, it is true that it does control the procedure of law-making in large measure. The expert ministerial bureaucracy drafts and initiates almost all important bills, adapts them to local and state needs through the second chamber (another bureaucratically composed body), steers them through *Bundestag* committees by its presence and powerful influence there, and subsequently, of course, oversees their administration. In the course of this process, Parliament has made little use so far of the possibilities of surveillance and criticism which the Constitution and its own standing orders provide.

A similar erosion, or lack of use of parliamentary power and influence, constantly threatens the new or semidemocratic countries. One of the characteristics of the mass party, as we have seen, is its dependence on its leader or leaders; the very effort of nation-making and of attempting to assert a new importance in international affairs encourages use of the legislative body as a sounding board rather than as a critic. The lack of administrative training and experience which handicaps legislators everywhere is most obvious in capitals like Jakarta, Colombo, Ft. Lamy, and Mexico City. This is not to say that the legislators in these and similar countries do not work hard (for they do), but rather that the combination of responsiveness to public attitudes and needs and of detailed supervision of executive action which is the mark of the better members of mature legislatures requires a sense of judgment and of overriding loyalty to the state uncommonly difficult to acquire in countries only gradually emerging from caste, or tribal, or family-oriented social structures.

Some of the difficulties resulting from allegiance to local rather than national interests are illustrated even in the American Congress. A congressman's party affiliation may be less important than the area from which he comes or the special interests in his constituency. This can lead not only to "logrolling" in the passage of legislation, but also to somewhat erratic and even arbitrary supervision of executive action, as has been true of the use of certain investigatory committees. Moreover, the power of congressional committees, especially in finance, seriously limits the ability of the executive to present a coordinated program. That none of these factors provides any insuperable obstacles either to efficient or to responsible government is obvious from the operations of American government; but similar sectionalism in less unified and mature countries can all too easily lead either to a frustrated administration or, as its corollary, authoritarianism.

What emerges from these comparisons is the fact that some of the frequently criticized defects of the British Parliament (and also of the Canadian and Australian Parliaments) are responsible, at least in part, for their freedom from the confusion, irresponsibility, and deadlock with which the French legislature of the Fourth Republic was rightly charged, or the lack of effectiveness of parliamentary action found in Germany and even more in many of the newer countries. If the system of representation is less perfect in Great Britain, both in reflecting fewer shades of political opinion and in exaggerating the majority of the larger party, these very distortions provide a stronger and more stable government capable of introducing a comprehensive program and of carrying it through. Party discipline not only reinforces this stability, but contributes to the responsibility and the educational value of the British system. It is true that Sweden

Channels of Political Action

with its multiparty system similarly provides stable and understandable government; but this is largely because the party combinations which provide the executive do not fluctuate sharply (as was the case in France) and also because its party groups provide fairly clear-cut alternatives at election time. But if party members fail to vote as a unit, it is impossible for the voters either to understand or to judge the party's position; and there is no assurance that a party, once elected, will have either the desire or the power to carry out its promises to the voters. It is at this point, in particular, that the ultimate responsibility to the voters implicit in representative government links up with the legislature's role of supervision and restraint on the executive.

VI

POLITICAL LEADERSHIP AND ADMINISTRATION

Throughout our discussions of how to keep government responsible, we have constantly referred to the importance of political leadership. With the spectacular growth in the functions of government which has taken place in every advanced country, the power of the executive has grown proportionately. Since, as we have seen, the legislature is not well fitted to perform the tasks of framing and initiating (as distinct from criticizing) legislation, or to engage in comprehensive planning, these tasks inevitably fall to the relatively small group of political leaders and top-ranking administrators. Moreover, the leadership function presents in an acute form a basic problem of modern government: how to integrate the numerous and often dissenting groups and interests in our pluralistic societies and at the same time to check overly integrated or concentrated power. Liberal democracy can all too easily develop toward the anarchy of diverse and uncooperating groups, while undemocratic systems tend to develop into authoritarianism and even, ultimately, dictatorship. In both situations, the balance wheel is responsible leadership. Thus, the effort to develop and maintain responsible leadership is the most crucial one for the future of the modern democratic state with its mass electorate and vast multiplicity of tasks.

THE HEADSHIP OF THE STATE: THE LEADER "REIGNS"

Integration through leadership has a twofold aspect: symbolism and actual authority. Psychologists and sociologists may argue about why it is that every human political organization needs a unifying symbol with or through which it can identify itself as unique and differentiated from every other unit; but the fact is undeniable. The unifying symbol may be impersonal (e.g., the American Constitution in its symbolic character), but more frequently it is embodied in a person. The extreme case of personalized symbolic (and actual) leadership is the totalitarian distatorship, with its *Fuehrer,* its *Duce,* or its "Great Father and Leader," as the Soviet press used to label Stalin. But traditionalist instead of such "charismatic" leadership may be equally strong. Not only divine right but also modern constitutional monarchy is a case in point. It is perhaps no coincidence that fascism as well as Communism, both of which discard traditional in favor of new-style symbols, have been least successful where monarchy as an institution still has strong roots. Thus the British, or Dutch, or Swedish Crown, despite its lack of real political power, has proved an antidote to totalitarianism. Moreover, in countries as widely separated as Iran and Thailand, a popular monarch is providing the best hope for stability and for furthering the interests of the people.

This underlines the important function of a head of state, as distinguished from the head of government. Where constitutional monarchies exist, the function of the head of state is chiefly to symbolize and represent the nation, especially in its foreign relations. Without the monarchy, the Commonwealth of Nations might have disintegrated. But republican countries, lacking such a "given" head, face the problem of providing for a dignified headship which can be a unifying force. In France, the office of President, separated as it was from actual executive power, used to depend for its respect and importance on the personality of its holder, but under the Fifth Republic, De Gaulle not only has great national prestige but also wide reserve powers. In West Germany, the dignified restraint with which the first President of the new regime, Theodor Heuss, exercised his function, accounts in large measure for the high esteem this office now enjoys. In the United States, the head of state exercises so much actual executive power that both dignity and prestige are never lacking. Though the Constitution is usually considered the primary unifying symbol in the United States, the degree to which the combined head-of-state-chief-executive is the leader of the nation in the people's mind is sharply illustrated when a President dies in office or is struck by sudden illness.

But presidential systems face a serious practical problem: how to relieve the chief executive and political leader, whose tasks are already almost superhuman, from the additional time- and energy-consuming burden involved in his symbolic role? This is why even totalitarian regimes sometimes make use of a person other than the leader for the discharge of symbolic functions, e.g., the King under Italian Fascism, or the Chairman of the Presidium of the Supreme Soviet in the Soviet Union. In the United States, it has recently been suggested that the Vice President might assume some of the ceremonial functions of headship. But symbolic leadership, once vested in one office or person, is not so easily transferred. It involves more than legal or constitutional amendments; it involves the mind and the habits of a nation.

THE HEADSHIP OF THE GOVERNMENT: THE LEADER "RULES"

IN DEMOCRACIES

Even leaving aside the symbolic function of political leadership, there remains enough to render the job trying under any standards of efficient one-man performance. Such a leader, in a democracy, must lay down the essential lines of policy in every field of domestic and foreign affairs; he must determine basic lines of military policy even in peacetime; he must coordinate the innumerable agencies of what in most modern countries has become the biggest "business establishment," the executive branch of the government; ordinarily he must lead, and keep together, the majority party (or, in a multiparty system, one of the major parties); he must manage a sometimes hostile, sometimes (in terms of majorities and minorities) unstable, or sometimes (in terms of political discipline) anarchic legislature; he must deal with a vast variety of interest groups and be able to resist their often powerful pressures; he must, to be successful, be alert to, and yet manage, public opinion. He should be a spokesman capable of explaining the problems and policies of government in simple and effective terms. He must ordinarily be able to win an open, competitive election. In a parliamentary democracy he should be able to participate successfully in the give-and-take of debate. He should be able to guide cabinet meetings, reconcile divergent opinions, and preside over the formulation of policy. He should, in addition, be a good administrator, not in the sense of detailed technical competence, but in the ability to oversee the range of administrative activity and to supervise the coordination of policy.

IN DICTATORSHIPS

In contrast, the task of a totalitarian leader seems simpler. True, his job is still vast in terms of the top decisions to be made. The governmental machine to be organized and coordinated may be even vaster than in democracies, particularly where, as in the Soviet Union or in China, it involves planning and running the economy; as in democracies, it comprises policy-making in the vital fields of foreign affairs and defense. On the other hand, a totalitarian leader does not have to manage a genuine legislature with an opposition or a party with its own will and perhaps conflicting wings. Everything, in this respect, is "coordinated." He does not have to deal with free-ranging, independent pressure groups though pressures, even dangerous ones, may work behind the scenes. If he must interpret policy to the masses, he does so unimpeded by the interference of a critical opposition or press. His popularity can be created artificially by the officially directed instruments of a manipulated public opinion. Since no opposition is tolerated, he need never win an open election.

Still, it is easy to underestimate the job of a totalitarian dictator. Since in such a regime there is no formal system whereby he secures access to power, the leader must have attained his position through extralegal means (in the democratic sense). As we know from a study of the rise of a Hitler or a Stalin, these include brute force as well as devious scheming; terroristic propaganda and purges; manipulation of the masses, of important power groups, and of close friends and lieutenants. His rise thus involves a selectivity in which only the fittest, in the sense of the toughest, survive. And after having arrived at the summit, the leader must maintain himself through similar means, since he has no support through constitutional legality or traditionalist legitimacy. Moreover, though he does not have to respond to an independent public opinion, he must, through constant interpretation, maintain the "purity" and at least seeming consistency of the doctrine, so as never to leave any doubt about the basic standards—the "line"—of the regime. This, in the case of Soviet leadership, involves coordinating or even directing the lines of *all* Communist regimes if it is to maintain the doctrinal leadership it claims. Difficulties in this respect have recently become apparent in Soviet-Chinese relations.

THE TWO COMPARED

If quick and decisive action is what modern government requires above all else, then, some have argued, it is the authoritarian leaders—proved in cunning and ruthlessness and free from special pressures, constitutional inhibitions, and the need to conciliate genuine opinion—who are far better suited to such conditions than are the democratic leaders. Especially in the vital fields of foreign, defense, and economic policies, concentration of power unhampered by popular or parliamentary controls and free from the danger of periodic change of personnel may appear the better guarantor of efficiency. But such arguments are based on doubtful assumptions. As a matter of fact, the pressures and special influences which openly harry democratic leadership also play on totalitarian leadership, though they are better hidden behind a (temporarily) streamlined façade. This became amply apparent in the examination of the Nazi regime after its downfall. Efficiency may suffer from overconcentration of power, overorganization, flight from responsibility due to fear of reprisals in case something goes wrong, absence of criticism and, consequently, the possibility that vital information never reaches the top level. And finally—as was clearly revealed in the process of "de-Stalinization" in the Soviet Union—if unlimited power makes possible impressive feats like Soviet industrialization under Stalin or German blitz-rearmament under Hitler, it also opens the way to possible blunders of equal dimensions, such as Hitler's later foreign policy or strategy decisions, or Stalin's wholesale purges and his policies toward satellite nations.

If democracies are less likely to commit either feats or blunders on such a gigantic scale, it is nevertheless significant that one-man rather than group leadership has characterized most of them in recent times. This is the case not only in democracies having a presidential system, as in the United States, but also in many of those with a cabinet system (which, of course, implies collective leadership), as in Britain. And it is true not only for older countries but also for new or revamped systems, like those of India, Indonesia, Ghana, Tanganyika, or West Germany. In fact, it is chiefly in the backwaters of world politics, or in countries like permanently neutralized Switzerland which are artificially shielded from international pressures, that genuine group leadership survives. France used to be the exception which merely proved the rule, for the very fact that its Premiers were rarely able to provide forceful leadership under the Fourth Republic was a prime factor in weakening that country and preparing the way for the strong executive of De Gaulle's Fifth Republic.

PROBLEMS OF SELECTION, RESPONSIBILITY, AND SUCCESSION OF THE CHIEF EXECUTIVE

If it is one-man rather than group leadership which characterizes government in our century, this perhaps attests to the importance of speedy and decisive policy-making, especially in foreign and security affairs. This situation throws into high relief, however, the vital import of the selection and responsibility of the supreme holder of power, the process of succession, the selection and responsibility of his chief lieutenants, and the access which they and others have to the leader, whether democratic or dictatorial.

SELECTION AND RESPONSIBILITY

Turning first to the problem of the selection of a responsible leader, we find that it is democracies rather than dictatorships which are faced with difficult problems. Dictators are self-selective and, in a constitutional sense, irresponsible. Fascist doctrine states this frankly and even boasts of it; the leader is not answerable to "the whims of the masses" but only to "history." Communist theory, it is true, proclaims the responsibility of the leader to the masses whom, even in Leninist doctrine, he is not supposed to leave too far behind. But who decides? Who holds "the vanguard" to its proper task in the absence of institutionalized criticism and control? The revelations about Stalin revealed a leadership which cared little what the masses, even those of "class-conscious" proletarians, thought or desired. And if Stalin's rule has been attacked by his successors as a monstrous deviation, there seems little chance that, in the absence of procedures for the enforcement of responsibility, they will act differently in either real or alleged emergencies.

In democracies, on the other hand, the decisive constitutional rules and procedures aim at providing responsible leadership. Whether selection is through direct popular election, as in presidential systems, or indirect, as in parliamentary systems where the voting is for a parliamentary party whose leader then becomes head of the government, it is the essence of democracy that the leader thus receives a mandate to which he can be held because it is limited in time. Periodic elections, therefore, are still the indispensable foundation of democratic responsibility.

In a multiparty system like the French under the Fourth Republic, the mandate is less clear than in the British type of two-party system, for the voter does not even know which one among the leading politicians of the various parties will eventually emerge as premier. This problem was less serious than it might appear, however, because the French Cabinet acted as a group and thus under group policies rather than under one-man leadership, while the French Parliament exercised close control over executive leadership. Whatever disadvantages this had in other respects, it was certainly an effective device for holding the Premier and his colleagues responsible to the popular will, which supposedly resided in the Assembly. This latter check is always a strong factor in the British system, for although the Prime Minister is in many respects in control of Parliament, that body retains, as we have emphasized, the important function of criticism.

On the surface, there is less enforceable responsibility in the presidential system. The American President is free from direct legislative control (though he must work closely with Congress to have his program accepted), and also from the restraints which the collegiate (or cabinet) system provides even in Britain. In this situation, the time limit of his term remains the only vital formal check. Certain informal or less institutionalized ways of rendering account to the public have developed, however, such as the presidential press conference and even the "fireside chat." These attest to the significant role which the press and other channels of mass communications play in modern democracy. Indeed, what would even parliament be in our times without newspapers, radio, and TV reporting to a mass audience on its debates and criticism?

Yet however effective the devices for checks, limitations, and enforcement of responsibility may be in democracies, the job, and therewith necessarily the power, of leadership remain uncomfortably great. This is the more so because of the necessity of granting an even less limited and less clearly defined power to government and, in particular, to the chief executive in time of crisis when only such concentrated power seems able to cope with the emergency. Especially in our times of cataclysmic threats and fears, the temptation to resort to speedy and decisive action is great, and there are few nations, even among the democracies, where emergency powers, martial-law powers, or whatever they may be called, are not tacitly or explicitly provided for. A political theorist, Carl Schmitt, has gone so far as to declare that internal sovereignty belongs to whoever can exercise emergency powers. It is perhaps significant that this author is German, for it has been in countries with weak democratic traditions that constitutions have most easily been overthrown or undermined through the use or abuse of emergency powers. But no matter how strong its democratic tradition, no country can afford to disregard the dangers inherent in this problem.

SUCCESSION

If democracies have more problems than dictatorships in selecting leaders, it is the other way around when it comes to succession to leadership positions. In all systems where law in fact, and not merely in form, determines what happens in government, succession will proceed in prescribed ways. In a monarchy, succession laws designate the heir to a throne; in any working democracy, the constitution or ordinary statutory law performs the same function in regard to presidents, prime ministers, or other leaders. Ordinarily, in such situations the transition from one leader to another thus proceeds without difficulty. In most democracies, of course, such a change happens in the normal course of regular constitutional procedures as a result of periodic elections.

In dictatorships, on the other hand, succession poses a problem of the very existence of the regime concerned. Since such rule is commonly based upon the "infallible," "unique," and, therefore, "irreplaceable person" of the one and only leader, it is put to its greatest test with his demise. Actually, neither Nazi nor Fascist dictatorships lived to pass this test, since the demise or overthrow of the leader was caused by the forcible action of foreign enemies. If there is an internal revolt, as in Cuba or Argentina, it means either the end of the dictatorship as such or the establishment of a new one on the basis of the successor's own "charisma."

Political Leadership and Administration

But after a dictator's demise, as with Lenin in 1924, and Stalin in 1953, the transmission of his halo to a successor is a difficult task. It might be facilitated by a formal sanction already given to the future successor by the dictator during his own lifetime, but this creates a "crown-prince problem," and totalitarian leaders, from Mussolini and Hitler to Stalin, have been loath to take such action. Franco, on the other hand, has long prepared to meet this problem, not by selecting a successor to the dictatorship, but rather through preparing for a return of the monarchy. In Stalin's case (assuming his death was natural) transmission of power was relatively smooth on the surface, but, as we now know, it involved a series of struggles for power before Khrushchev emerged as the undisputed leader. Beria was killed; Malenkov greatly demoted; Molotov exiled to Siberia for some time and kept under constant supervision; Marshal Zhukov and, later, Marshal Bulganin ousted from their positions of authority. What seems evident from past experience in the Soviet Union is that control of the party machinery is the best route to ultimate power, and that the tilting between power-conscious figures within the party hierarchy may cause the rise and fall of many individual aspirations before the ultimate contest for succession takes place.

If, as is obvious, the sharpest contrasts over succession are between dictatorial and democratic regimes, it should also be noted that different types of constitutional systems produce their own characteristic ways of providing for the succession of their leaders. The presidential elections in the American system provide not only the chief executive but, simultaneously, the leader of the party whose nominee is installed in the White House; though most American Presidents have had experience as members of Congress, or slightly more often, as state governors, neither is mandatory, as was proved by General Eisenhower's election in 1952. In the British type of parliamentary government, in contrast, the Prime Minister is the leader of the party which wins a majority of the seats; inevitably, he has had parliamentary experience and, almost inevitably (Winston Churchill proved an exception), he has headed the party organization for a considerable time.

A party leader may be chosen by the parliamentary members of the party, as is the practice in Great Britain, Australia, New Zealand, and South Africa, or by a party convention, as is done in Canada or, commonly, in Continental European countries. In either case, it takes a major palace revolution to unseat him once he is selected. It is true that the Canadian Progressive Conservative Party picked three leaders in a space of sixteen years, hoping each time to find one who could lead them to victory, as did John Diefenbaker in 1957, to end a twenty-two year period of office by the Liberals; the Australian Labour Party twice renounced its leaders, once during World War I and once in the depression, when they were already serving as Prime Ministers, but in both instances it was the party, not the leaders, who lost office. But these are exceptions, as was Churchill's elevation to office in 1941, and normally the leaders of conservative, liberal, and labor parliamentary parties have long tenures of office. Thus, they bring to the highest executive office, when they achieve it, a breadth of experience in parliamentary and party affairs which few American Presidents can rival.

Moreover, the parliamentary system grooms the next aspirant for office through the grueling responsibilities of leading the opposition. This is a function for which the American system has no parallel. In a half-hearted way, Adlai Stevenson was accepted as spokesman for the Democratic Party after his two unsuccessful candidacies for President, but in 1960, the party turned to a new figure, John F. Kennedy. Thus, paradoxically, the system which, potentially, vests the greatest authority of any democratic country in a single figure does least to provide training and experience for those responsibilities.

In an imaginative effort to combine personal leadership with a close working-together of the executive and legislature, Ghana's republican Constitution, adopted in 1960, and said to be framed by Nkrumah himself, provides that the President shall be both head of state and leader within parliament. He is chosen by the legislators, who must, in turn, avow their choice for President at any time they stand for office. The President may dissolve the legislature at any time, but in so doing he also terminates his own mandate. Thus, executive leadership and parliamentary stability are interrelated in an attempt to find a new means of ensuring, as all democracies must, that there is a regularized and known way of providing for the succession to the leader. The Bonn Constitution of West Germany, too, as has been seen, provides a novel device to avoid a political void by providing that a chief executive can be forced out only if a majority can agree on his successor.

Among the new countries, the problem of succession is made more difficult by the relatively small number of people capable of assuming such responsibilities. Any country may have a charismatic leader—and in any system the demands on and the response to leadership will depend greatly on whether the leader is charismatic or not—but the importance of personality is particularly great where there is little sense of national unity and the party structure is fairly rudimentary. Instead of being organizational, as in more developed democracies, leadership in the new states tends to be personal and even self-selected (but rather through ability to hold conflicting groups together than through a struggle for power). The steady disintegration of the Moslem League and its inability to provide coherent direction in Pakistan after the death of one leader and the assassination of another illustrates the particular dependence of party organization on leadership in newly developing states. Not only is there a disturbing reliance on one or a few leaders to hold together political organization and to direct development, but, almost as a corollary which reflects the uncertainty about the succession, a degree of haste in achieving results which may threaten constitutional procedures. In both respects, the crucial period is the early years of independence, and if these are successfully negotiated, the country may acquire a more stable social unity and more settled patterns of action able to survive the strains and divisions which, as we have seen, have tilted the balance toward at least temporary army rule in several Asian countries and the Sudan.

THE SELECTION AND RESPONSIBILITY OF LIEUTENANTS

The differences between the ways democratic and totalitarian states select political lieutenants are even more striking than are those in the selection of chief executives. Where political lieutenants obviously share power, as do the members of the cabinet in parliamentary systems, they are formally appointed by the chief executive or (as is the case in Australia when the Labour Party is in office) selected by the caucus, i.e., the parliamentary members of the party. Under the doctrine of collective responsibility, everyone in the cabinet not only considers but also must publicly support government policy. If a minister wishes to oppose a policy outside the walls of the cabinet chamber, he must resign to do so. As long as he is in office, however, he both runs his department and assumes full responsibility for its policies before parliament and the public. The American Cabinet is also composed of political heads of departments, but it is a pale reflection of the British or Australian Cabinet as far as sharing power is concerned, for the extent of its members' responsibilities and policy-making depends on the will of the particular President. Under President Eisenhower, for example, John Foster Dulles had virtually unlimited discretion in the foreign-affairs field, while his successor, Christian Herter, had relatively little. Cabinets in multiparty systems like that of the Fourth French Republic reflect impermanent coalitions, but for this very reason a minister may possess more independent authority than a British cabinet minister, since in the multiparty system he is usually not only an individual of competence, but also the representative of a party whose support is essential to the life of the coalition. Moreover, in the field of foreign affairs, for example, the tenure of office of a minister in the Fourth French Republic was often far longer than that of the Premier. Under the Fifth Republic, the concentration of power in the executive, the fact that a minister may not retain a seat in the legislature, and the tendency to use civil servants as ministers, have produced a situation in which the French Cabinet is more like the American than the British, while the chambers are far less vigorous than in either of the other two countries. The same holds for West Germany, where the Chancellor has appointed, shifted, and dismissed ministers with little concern for either Parliament or his own party.

In totalitarian states, lieutenants to the dictator occupy a far more equivocal position than do cabinet members in democratic states. Their selection is a reflection of the internal power struggle at a given moment. Even when the dictator seems to occupy an unquestioned position of authority, shifts go on—as was seen throughout Stalin's regime—which exalt one person temporarily and then cause his disappearance or demotion. China is notable for the constancy with which its top figures, in particular Mao Tse-tung and Chou En-lai, have worked together, but most other non-Soviet Communist states have felt the impact of the permanent purge or of the struggle for ultimate succession all the way to the highest levels.

THE ROLE AND SELECTION OF THE BUREAUCRACY

The higher bureaucracy is as important in providing advice, aid, and also policy proposals as is the second line of executive leadership, the ministers. No man can hope to keep abreast of the multitudinous factors of modern administration. One of the most important talents a leader must have is the ability to delegate powers, although, if he is to fulfill his mandate from the people, he must also retain ultimate responsibility. The chief executive is also and necessarily the head of the administration. But in democratic states, the administration carries not only the responsibility of executing the laws, but also of seeing that they fulfill the purposes for which they were designed. Thus the administration, and particularly the higher bureaucracy, must be constantly alert both to the purposes of the political leaders of the country and to the needs as well as desires of the public.

This view of the role of the bureaucracy, which is now generally accepted in democratic states, was disputed in earlier times. The Prussian and subsequently Imperial German view was that serving the purposes of the state rather than providing services for the people was the primary duty of public administration. This concept had the advantage of establishing clear-cut and single-minded responsibility to the monarch, and it was saved from promoting arbitrary authoritarianism by the insistence on the *Rechtsstaat,* the rule of law. It has been one of the reasons why, to this day, the ministerial bureaucracy in West Germany dominates in many political processes, and especially vis-à-vis the legislature. But this view fitted ill with the notions of popular sovereignty characteristic of the French Revolution. Under their impact, law came to be regarded not merely as the will of the state, enunciated by its supreme figure, but as a collection of rules devised for the better organization of the affairs of the community. In this perspective, public power became transmuted into public service.

In France, syndicalism went a step further, maintaining that public employees were no different from private employees and should have the right, therefore, to organize in trade unions, engage in political activity, and publicly express their opinions even if these were contrary to those of the political leaders. But activities along these lines were among the factors which weakened Italy and Spain in the early interwar period and facilitated the accession of authoritarianism; they were not without effect in undermining the postwar Fourth French Republic. What may be termed the public-service state, at least in countries following the Anglo-Saxon tradition, now, therefore, endorses these views: that the interests of the public are superior to those of any group of public servants; that employment by the state differs from private employment in the techniques and tactics which it is legitimate to use in attempting to change conditions of service (in particular, strikes are not an acceptable means of pressure); and that, while government employees should have the right to exercise the franchise in their private capacities, there is a basic incompatibility between government employment and open political activity, at least at the level of government (i.e., local or national) in which service is being rendered.

These distinctions make much less sense in jobs comparable to those in private service, it must be admitted, than in jobs that are unique to public service. In cases where some sectors of the economy are nationalized, there would seem little reason for treating their employees differently than would be the case if the services were privately supported—except for the fact that nationalization either creates or grows out of monopolies and often in spheres which provide essential public services, like transportation. Thus a strike in a nationalized industry or service, like coal mining or air transportation, has far more impact on the country as a whole than would a strike against an individual enterprise. Nonetheless, as government spreads into new areas of activity, there is increasing reason to separate what might be called genuine public-law and basically private-law employment and to treat them differently. Few people can doubt, however, that special provisions and traditions are essential for the type of government employment for which there is no parallel in business.

But if there is agreement on this fact, there are wide differences in the ways democratic states have handled problems of selection, training, and promotion, particularly for that all-important group, the higher bureaucracy, which is involved in policy-making almost as much as in administration. The British deliberately recruit personnel for particular types of responsibilities and select most candidates for the top grades with the help of written and oral tests which seek to evaluate the intellectual capacities and character of outstanding university graduates. Unlike most other countries—except those of the older and some of the newer members of the Commonwealth overseas—the British choose the highest departmental officials from the permanent service, thus making it a career service of great distinction, although they run the possible danger of substituting ability for genuine sympathy with the programs being introduced. Americans, on the other hand, have never wholly discarded their belief that practical experience in business or commerce may be more useful in government service than academically tested ability and long experience. Although it is more common these days to find top officials retaining their posts (particularly posts requiring technical skills) despite a change in administration, there is far more infiltration from outside into all ranks of government service than is the case in Great Britain or in European countries. This can be particularly valuable when a "new deal" is instituted and knowledge is combined with enthusiasm in those most concerned with introducing new measures, but it also limits the attractiveness of public service as a career. Moreover, the number of short-term "political" appointments, particularly under Republican administrations, makes decisiveness and continuity of policy difficult. The French use academic tests based on specialized training for their higher administrators (who often perform tasks delegated to the executive, or "sergeant-major" level of British administration, as well as more characteristically directive ones, simply because the French service is less strong at the second-highest level), but a minister brings with him his own "cabinet" of administrators who work with the regular departmental officials to see that the minister's policies are carried out in accordance with his wishes.

Other, more subtle differences may result from the class structure and the prestige of the higher civil service. If, as was long true in Great Britain, ministers and the higher bureaucracy come from the same families, schools, and universities, they tend to have the same implicit assumptions about how policy should be executed; the British Labour Party found it could also work well with the higher civil servants, however, when it came into office. But the degree of national consensus on essentials which this fact reflected did not exist in Weimar Germany, where the permanent service hampered, when it did not impede, the implementation of democratically inclined or socially advanced policies, and thus contributed to that regime's weakness and ultimate collapse in 1933. The less class-conscious and more equalitarian American educational system leads to a more differentiated, if less intellectually inclined, higher public service than exists in Great Britain, France, or Germany; if this has the advantage of representativeness, it can hardly balance the limitations of less marked ability.

The prestige a bureaucracy enjoys also has a bearing on the type of person it is able to attract. In Germany, the public official has a higher status than in any other European country, or possibly any place else, both a reflection of a belief in the expert and an identification of bureaucracy with the state. In Sweden, Denmark, and Holland, he is trusted, but he is not regarded with anything like the same deference. The Swiss, French, Italians, and Spanish are openly critical of their public servants, though the latter two with more reason than the former. Americans, with their traditional idealization of the businessman, are only gradually acquiring the degree of respect for public service which the British have long held, and learning, too, that such respect and the standards of the service reinforce each other.

If such factors are so influential, can it be said that the higher civil service is ever neutral in its attitudes toward public questions? Perhaps not; but should it be? The kind of issues dealt with by the top level of bureaucrats for the most part are not those which can be handled by reference to rules. They are policy-raising issues for which no legisture and no executive can provide all the directives. Higher civil servants are confronted constantly by the need to use their own discretion in determining how best to carry out a policy so that its results will be in the public interest. This necessitates a sensitivity to tensions within the community and to genuine needs, as opposed to spurious claims, which taxes every faculty. The best members of the higher bureaucracy are likely to be those who are not hidebound either by ideology or by special class interests, public servants who can retain an open mind and a sympathetic comprehension of public needs and purposes. If, as is true in democratic states, the public servant is immediately responsible to the elected executive, the ultimate responsibility of both is to the people.

BUREAUCRACY IN THE NEW STATES

Nowhere are administrative skill, experience, and public responsibility more needed than in the new states. Their very poverty of material resources and accumulated capital thrusts upon them a multitude of tasks in their efforts to become "modern." Almost all these tasks must be directed or supervised by the public service. Yet it is commonly in this field that their lacks are greatest. The five hundred top Indian administrators who, up to the time India attained independence, shared the subcontinent's major governmental responsibilities with an equal number from Great Britain itself, perhaps constituted the most valuable heritage of British rule in India. That Pakistan could claim only about seventy of those who had been trained for high posts under British rule made its task of administrative construction a major difficulty and contributed to the laxities which paved the way for army rule. That India had over four hundred to depend on vastly aided its early years of independence and its ambitious development projects. Compared to both these countries, those which have been achieving independence in Africa have been handicapped indeed. The Africanization of administrative services did not start on any scale until after World War II, and, in all too many cases, has been hastened at the expense of training and quality.

Strikingly enough, Ghana, which has some of the best African administrative talent, also had more white employees in its public service three years after achieving independence than before 1957, reflecting the fact that African advance could not keep up with the expansion of responsibilities caused by large-scale development. When the Belgians in the Congo withdrew from their responsibilities so hastily to grant independence in June, 1960, the most serious lack there was that of African administrators. In the British and French territories in Africa, arrangements have commonly been made with former colonial officials to remain in office until Africans were trained to take their places; in the Congo, the lack of confidence on both sides led to premature withdrawal. The fact that the United Nations had to step in not only to re-establish order, but also to restart essential services

Political Leadership and Administration

points to the importance of establishing a substantial international civil service to aid the developing countries.

The new states face special handicaps in building their administrative services. Their educational structures taper quickly to the point of the pyramid; in other words, even where primary education is widespread, as is increasingly the case, secondary and higher educational facilities remain minimal. Those who succeed in completing secondary education frequently go on through university, thereby increasing the numbers available for professional posts in the administration, but leaving almost no one to fill the highly important secondary rung of executive and even secretarial posts. A further problem arises from the need to replace traditional family-oriented loyalties by loyalty to the state. Traditional norms in many non-Western societies dictate what we condemn as nepotism, that is, providing jobs for family members; public money and private money are also less sharply differentiated. Particularly in Africa, there is the further problem that when one member of a family has a well-paid post, his relatives anticipate that he will support them.

The colonial bureaucracies have set a high standard of probity and devotion to duty which countries like Nigeria expect their own administrators to follow. The transfer of authority to local hands requires a major adjustment in the thinking of the most upright bureaucracy, however, for independence not only means a local center of power; it also means that bureaucracy is responsible to that center of power instead of having virtually unlimited discretion in its own hands. Thus, even where administrative skills exist, the new states have their own particular problems in developing the kind of relationship between the elected executive and the public administration that befits a democratically organized state. In the light of all these difficulties and of the great pressures for development, it is the achievements of the new states rather than their shortcomings which should be highlighted.

BUREAUCRACY IN TOTALITARIAN STATES

Totalitarian states face an inherent dilemma in regard to their administrative services. They depend on them far more than would any democratic state, particularly if the latter has a mature economy within which private enterprise assumes a major role. Their very dependence on administrators to manage the economy as well as all other services, however, runs contrary to the concentrations of power in the hands of the party. Moreover, efficient administration dictates its own rules of organization, i.e., fixed jurisdictions, hierarchical chain of command, reliance on written orders, dependence on specialists, and stable routines. Yet this regularity contrasts sharply with the pressures of what we have called the permanent purge. In other words, the two major means whereby totalitarian states, and in particular the Soviet Union, control all aspects of life—the bureaucracy and the party—require opposing conditions for their maximum effectiveness: the former, stability; the latter, constant ferment.

These counterpulls have evidenced themselves throughout the history of the Soviet Union. Marxist dogma, of course, condemned bureaucracy as an instrument of bourgeois oppression. Lenin originally thought the workers themselves would be able to administer the state and industry. Since the importance of administrative skills and responsibility quickly became apparent in the Soviet state, however, party members were assigned to watch over managerial operations. Under the Five-Year Plans, through

Political Leadership and Administration

which the great industrial expansion of the Soviet Union has taken place, professional administrators began to achieve a privileged status, and they became important party members. Even then, however, they suffered periodically from impossible demands and from the fear of punishment for failure to meet them. In order to fulfill their quotas, ministries would try to corral supplies, transport, and labor. Khrushchev himself is our authority on some of the resulting absurdities which led to duplication of effort in some instances and lack of use of resources in others (such as one ministry moving goods in its own ships in one direction only and allowing them to return empty when another ministry was doing exactly the same in the opposite direction). Khrushchev's own administrative reorganization in 1957 sought to avoid such wastage by breaking up the top-heavy ministries centralized in Moscow under the Stalinist regime and placing the direction of industry under the 105 regions into which the country is divided. Still more important from his point of view, however, the reorganization undercut the power of the managerial class, broke up the bureaucratic concentration in the capital, and brought industry under the control of his own well-entrenched regional party agents. As with so many other policies which Khrushchev has promoted, this one was designed to enhance the power of the party by simplifying its task of maintaining supervision over the economic bureaucracy, that is, that part of the administration which directs industry. Yet inevitably, the new administrative patterns which developed are also solidifying. Thus the contest continues, with ultimate political power firmly vested in party hands, but the rationale of a heavily bureaucratized state exerting its own constant pressures toward stability.

INFORMAL CHANNELS OF ACCESS TO THE LEADER

In a period when government seems to consist so largely of impersonal regulations applied to vast numbers of similar cases and situations, it may appear strange to put great weight on questions like these: Who has the ear of a president? Who is most influential in the cabinet surrounding a prime minister? We expect camarillas to play their role in uncontrolled dictatorships, but in other systems stories of personal influence and intrigue in high places, of "gray eminences," and ruling mistresses seem to belong to the past, with dynastic and similar personal rule. Yet personal friendship, kitchen cabinets, and similar influences have never ceased to play a role in democratic as well as in dictatorial systems. The problem has indeed gained new significance with the heightened tasks of political leadership and the increased urgency and secrecy surrounding it in the age of nuclear insecurity.

The area of governmental secrecy has grown increasingly for security and related reasons. The top level of policy-making has, of course, always been conducted in secrecy, even in the most developed democracies, as witness the meetings and discussions of the British Cabinet, or those of the American "Cabinet" and National Security Council. This is inevitable if there is to be free and frank discussion before policy decisions are taken.

But while participation in such bodies is highly important, we discover from time to time that their members are not necessarily those whose words will be most influential on ultimate decisions. Department or agency heads in the United States or even cabinet ministers in Great Britain may be less influential, in practice, than unofficial aides, friends, or lieutenants, especially where, despite the enormous growth of his functions and powers, the leader is not provided with an appropriate official staff of his own. More important than top-ranking official advisers may be secretaries, appointment officers, or special or personal assistants, like a Sherman Adams in Washington or a Hans Globke at Bonn. The mere fact of a chief executive's limited time points up the problem. Policy decisions may depend on the appointment calendar, that is, on who gains access to the holder of power and who does not, or on what the leader hears and reads and what he does not. Connected with this is the problem which looms so large these days—how best to coordinate "intelligence." The leader can absorb only so much; what is selected, and in what form it is presented, may determine his action or inaction, with far-reaching results. In place of emphasizing the vast powers of the leader in a modern, industrial state, some observers see the chief executive, perhaps particularly in the United States, as the prisoner of his staff. All the more reason, therefore, to give executives the maximum aid by highly responsible assistants, and to encourage the kind of inquisitiveness into the wide range of governmental affairs which keeps ultimate decision-making in the hands of those to whom the public has entrusted that responsibility.

THE ROLE OF PRESSURE GROUPS

The problem of the influence exercised upon key men, particularly the top figures in the executive and the administration, is far more complex, however, than these comments may seem to indicate. Every administration, whether democratic or dictatorial, has its own internal rivalries, strains, and divisions of opinion. Some of these derive from self-seeking, some from genuine differences of view about the public interest, some from overspecialization, and others from lack of knowledge and experience; and a few, though these may be particularly important, are the result of outside influences and pressures. One objective of democracies is to bring these influences and pressures out into the open, so that their source and impact can be evaluated more fairly. This is not to say, as some people have, that pressure groups are necessarily harmful because they seek to exalt the interest of small, though possibly very wealthy or highly organized segments of the population above those of the whole group. It is rather intended to emphasize that public responsibility requires the maintenance of sufficient openness about how political and administrative decisions are reached so that undue influence can be corrected.

Pressure groups, in fact, have become something of a fifth estate in the American system of government and exert rather more influence in other democratic countries than is customarily realized. They form a link between the people and government of which most administrators make use to secure information on attitudes and facts. Any democratic government would expect, for example, to consult farmers' organizations before instituting new farm programs and also for evaluating existing ones. The problem created by pressure groups is not that they are consulted, but that they sometimes force their will upon legislators or administrators and thereby not only lower standards of public morality but also distort to their own advantage policy which is or should be designed for the public interest.

It is not without reason that the most detailed studies of pressure groups have been of those which operate on the American scene. The American party system, with its lack of centralization (except at election time), of discipline, and of firm leadership, lends itself to the pressures of special-interest groups. So, too, does the separation of powers, which opens the way to exploiting not only rivalries, but what is often a disturbing lack of communication and integration between, and even within, the different branches. Moreover, the public passively acquiesces, for the most part, in the open tug of war between rival interest groups and, in what may be still more costly, alliances between them through which potentially conflicting claims are resolved in a manner detrimental to the public interest. Management and labor, for example, might agree on large wage increases, but such an agreement could run counter to the interests of consumers in preventing higher prices and consequent inflationary pressures; lobbies may combine in order to raise tariffs, with some of the same results. This process is commonly expected and accepted without much public analysis, except sporadically, of its effects.

Because economic concentration has gone so far in the United States—some 135 corporations owned 45 per cent of the industrial assets of the country in 1951, which amounted in turn to nearly one-quarter of the manufacturing of the whole world—there is constant suspicion among liberals that political power is subject to economic power, whether exercised through open lobbying or through the influence of the "dollar-a-year" men who contribute their services to the administration, or through dubious practices. According to the Communists, of course, government in a capitalistic economy inevitably becomes an instrument in the hands of dominant economic interests and the political leaders, the "running dogs" of the bourgeoisie. While this view grossly exaggerates the impact of economic power, there can be little question that corporate wealth does influence the power of government. In Great Britain, France, and Germany, as well as the United States, administrators find it more convenient to consult with big business and its representatives than with the multitude of small ones. The organizations of the former are more streamlined, their information more clearly defined, their actions more predictable. Beyond this, the resources of big corporations make it possible to exert pressure on the many rungs of the American administrative and legislative processes. So, too, do the resources of the big labor unions, some of which have as marked a concentration of authority as do corporations.

It is significant to note that interest groups may also exert pressure for change through the judicial system, the most striking example being the successful effort of the National Association for the Advancement of Colored People to secure the judgment by the Supreme Court that the segregation of schools is unconstitutional. On the whole, however, pressure groups concentrate on the administrative bureaus or ministries and on committee chairmen and party leaders. Many of the proposals for new public policy come from such pressure groups, it must be noted, but on balance it seems as if pressure politics had less effect through causing innovations than through preventing change. The long campaign against national health insurance in the United States is a classic example of the latter process.

If the party and governmental systems in the United States facilitate the impact of private pressures on policy-making, the strength of the national consensus limits their divisive effect. But in France under the Fourth Republic, the situation was more serious. The growing lack of discipline in the political parties, other than the Communists, opened the way for an ever-increasing influence by pressure groups, particularly those of the business lobby, until at times it surpassed that of the parties themselves, while the lack of public agreement on political and social values provided a milieu in which conflict became exaggerated rather than resolved. In Great Britain, in contrast, a highly structured bureaucracy and highly disciplined political parties keep the decision-making process firmly in control, and pressure groups become a major means of keeping constantly in touch with a wide variety of attitudes toward public policy.

It is apparent, therefore, that the role of pressure groups in the political system is largely determined by the strength or weakness of the political decision-making process. Lobbying can claim to follow two essentially democratic procedures: the right to participate in the formulation of policy and the right to redress of grievances. So long as pressure groups are not permitted to usurp the political function, their specialized knowledge of attitudes and facts can provide an important link between government and the people to whom it is responsible.

It is here that the type and attitude of leadership will be decisive. Especially in a country like the United States, where the parties are the chief representatives of competing interests, the national mandate of the Presidency is of utmost importance. If there is no integration of the plurality of groups and interests at this point, there will be none at all. Still, the American system, where interests, although working in and through parties, are not organized *as* parties, is at an advantage compared with systems where coalition governments made up from interest parties have a hard time rising above a mere dividing up of the commonwealth in their own favor.

Much also depends, in this connection, upon the social origin of the political elite. In countries where, as until recently in Britain and still largely in Germany, political leadership is restricted to an educated class drawn from a relatively small upper stratum, leadership easily identifies national interest with that of narrower groups and classes. But this is not necessarily the case. Not infrequently, a feeling of *noblesse oblige* leads persons of aristocratic or similar upper-class backgrounds to act in a more broadminded, liberal, and even democratic way than those from a lower stratum would do. This has been true in America, too. More democracy in the selection of the political elite has not always resulted in less personal, social, or similar bias. Also, while European countries may display class restrictions in selection, the "classless" society of the United States still manifests actual, though not legal, restrictions based on racial origin or religious affiliation.

A free world engaged in competition with a system where a jungle type of struggle for political survival tends to bring the most ruthless to the fore can hardly afford to place restrictions on the selection of the ablest among its citizens. It is, therefore, confronted with a twofold educational problem: first, how to educate the citizenry so that, free from bias and unaffected by the hullabaloo of the hucksters, it will make intelligent choices; and second, in what amounts to a modern version of the age-old problem of the "education of the prince," how to develops in its potential leaders that combination of knowledge and ability out of which they will act both with authority and with responsibility, the hallmarks of democratic leadership.

VII

BELIEF SYSTEMS AND POLITICS

THE ROLE OF IDEOLOGY

At the beginning of this book, we pointed out that the deepest challenge of totalitarianism lies in its claim that it alone can fill the spiritual void left by the decline of established religion in the modern age. Beyond their material wants, men need a belief in the meaningfulness of their lives, a faith in some higher cause to which they as individuals as well as the groups to which they belong can be devoted. Many believe that in this period of change and crisis, liberal democracy is failing to answer this need.

Behind these issues lies another problem. It can be summed up in these questions: What ties political communities together? What is it that forms those feelings and attitudes of attachment to the group, that minimum of allegiance without which a political community can neither be established nor endure? Particularly in our time of numerous and strongly divisive views, interests, and even centers of allegiance, what gives cohesion to a political community?

We in the West have long ignored this problem, largely because we have been under the influence of that mainstream of modern social and political thought: individualism. Whether it bases itself upon the concept of an original social or political contract, or upon the concept of utility, individualism has assumed that political units like nation-states are founded upon, or could and should be founded upon, the free and voluntary association of self-determining, rational, enlightened human beings.

But nearly two centuries ago, Burke pointed out that a country is more than a utilitarian or contractual association; that its cohesion rests less on interests and is less braced by reason than it is founded on custom and tradition; and that even prejudice may serve to preserve "the ancient order into which we are born." To many moderns this may sound like tribalism; but even Rousseau, who differed from Burke in so many respects, called for a "civil religion" so that the "general will" of a free community would be sure to prevail.

To talk of maintaining or even instilling the right prejudices, or of enforcing a civil religion, points up a basic dilemma in the relations between the individual and the community. We have been apt to forget that the attempt to render the individual autonomous and to make him the foundation of free communities and limited government has been relatively rare and recent in history. For most of the history even of Western Europe, and of most of the world until the present or the recent past, political communities, however they were first established (i.e., by war, by conquest, or occasionally by free compact), have been kept together by an unquestioning, traditionalist allegiance of the ruled to the rulers. Generally, there was no conscious effort to indoctrinate the people, nor even to mold their attitudes and opinions through formal education; this was not necessary. It was the prevailing atmosphere, the transmitted value and belief systems, which provided these standards. And it was in large part the churches which provided whatever institutional and organizational apparatus was required to ensure their hold.

With the era of the Enlightenment came a change in attitude. To many people it seemed desirable to conduct human affairs on the basis of conscious, deliberate, and free acceptance of value standards, whether they eventually turned out to be religious or not. Loyalty freely given provides a stronger and more democratic foundation of nations than does an enforced allegiance—or even a less consciously and more traditionally established allegiance. Thus, such loyalty has become the truly democratic ideal.

Frequently, however, it is only the few who know how to develop their own personal beliefs and how to make these beliefs the basis of living together with others in political communities. This explains why it is that after traditional rulership has lost its grip, it is often a new irrational emotion, nationalism, which has ensured the cohesion of existing units or has made for the formation of new ones. When nationalism was simply a moderate and relatively calm feeling of belonging to that group which constitutes the nation, it could still be reconciled with a liberal-democratic individualism. But to the extent that nationalism became the substitute religion of those who needed or were instilled with more extreme and fervent feelings of attachment, it became a focal point for emphatic identification with one group, and antagonism, even hatred, toward all others. Thus nationalism has all too easily been converted into an ideology of exclusivism and, in a variety of forms (racialism, bellicism, imperialism, Social Darwinism, political romanticism), has eventually become the doctrinal foundation of various totalitarian movements, most particularly Italian Fascism and the even more extreme movement of Nazism.

Nationalism is one basis of modern totalitarian ideology. Another basis has been formed by the need for a coherent philosophy of government and politics, a political *Weltanschauung*, which arises once the masses of the people have been called upon to participate in politics. It is well known how this need contributed to the appeal of Nazism; but we should note that even in the nineteenth century it had led rising and unattached proletarian groups to embrace the new Marxian creed and movement, in Germany and elsewhere. And far more widely, as we know full well, have the crises, strains, and stresses of our century contributed to the appeal of this other major type of totalitarian ideology, Communism—particularly since this latter philosophy has a rational or quasi-rational appeal through its explanation of historical evolution and current conditions, which draws to it many who would reject the irrational mysticism and racial or nationalist dogmas of fascism.

But the yearning for a belief system and a movement with a cause can also be found in more Western and less extreme climes. It is observable in some degree in most mass parties, whether that of British Labour or the more leftist of French or Italian parties. It reflects the *anomie* (the lack of basic rules or standards of value) of individuals lost in the maze of modern mass society, who have become alienated from traditional ways of life without having found safe new ones.

Confronted with the weakening of social ties which

anomie represents in its most extreme form, democracy runs two opposite dangers. If it sticks to its liberal ideal and leaves the individual free to choose among standards and causes without direction, the plurality of interests and creeds of modern society may lead to such disunity as to endanger the cohesion of the political unit. In the extreme case, it may even lead to the internecine warfare of armed ideologies; or, at the least, result in sheer political opportunism, which is likewise a doubtful basis for national cohesion. The other and opposite danger is that the effort may be made to instill loyalty from above, to indoctrinate the citizen and especially the younger generation with whatever civil religion seems appropriate. This obviously leads to the evils of conformity and to the undermining of the liberalism with which democracy is so intimately bound.

To avoid the horns of this dilemma requires wise judgment and constant vigilance. The middle way between the two extremes is made easier where nations enjoy the absence of deep class divisions, the maturity of a people used to developing its own standards, and relative security from outside dangers. Here the impact of international developments is obvious. As long as nation-states still enjoyed a fair measure of security, they needed less emotional attachment on the part of their citizens for their internal cohesion than do present-day, more insecure units. In the absence of security, it is tempting to ensure an iron unity through uniformity of creed, a pattern perhaps less virulent than, but nevertheless with elements of, totalitarianism.

However, totalitarian regimes run into troubles of their own. There seems to be a law of diminishing returns in regard to indoctrination. Though individuals in a mass society long for safe beliefs, they are yet easily satiated when doctrines are too emphatically instilled or when, in the present conflict of systems and ideologies, one has replaced another in bewildering sequence.

Consider the case of the young Pole who told an American journalist (*New York Times,* May 11, 1956):

> When I was ten, I ceased to believe in my fatherland. I had God. When I was 15, I ceased to believe in God. . . . A friend gave me help. He was a Communist. He restored my faith in mankind. These were my happiest years. . . . Now it has turned out that what my family said about the dictatorship of Stalin was true. . . . I do not know how to change my soul for the fourth time. . . . I have no basis for believing anything. . . .

Such an experience can hardly fail to make an individual cynical or apathetic. He avoids taking sides or positions of responsibility; he will not be caught napping again. Such attitudes are especially common in countries which have gone through the experience of totalitarianism and its aftermath of nazification and denazification, of purges and counterpurges. But the problem is an even more general one, connected with the phenomenon of "de-politization." The less the individual in mass society retains a chance to control events, the less his political *and* his ideological concern; and—in an endless and vicious circle—the more frantic the ideological appeals of those actual or would-be rulers who feel the need for ever more fervent adherence. For totalitarian regimes this means increasing difficulty in binding the ruled indefinitely to their control. In its turn, democracy has to steer the difficult path between political apathy, creating what the French call *incivisme,* and the totalitarian temptations which are always present.

CHURCH AND STATE

Consideration of the role of ideologies in the modern political world inevitably brings us to the problem of the relation between church and state. While political science cannot presume to pass on the ultimate validity of religious truth, it can and indeed must recognize the existence of individual religious beliefs as objective facts and of organized religion as a socially and politically relevant institution. Needless to say, it is the political consequences of both individual belief and organized religion which are our proper concern here.

We may usefully return to the phenomenon of *anomie,* the lack of values of the individual in mass society, to understand the role religion plays in a modern nation and, in particular, the problems created by the sometimes conflicting demands of churches and the modern state. Industrialization, urbanization, and the resulting mechanization of life have confronted religion with new tasks which it can shun only at the risk of becoming a mere "Sunday creed" without vital commitment to, and connection with, modern life. If in the past religion served the social function of transmitting from generation to generation the generally accepted values, it can today assume the function of providing individuals who are lost in a directionless maze with new or new-old standards and thereby give direction and meaning to the lives of many who have failed to develop their own.

In assuming this responsibility, however, different religions may follow different paths, and it is important, in relating them to the state and to politics, to understand these differences. Protestantism, for instance, turns primarily to the individual and asks him to turn to the word of God and interpret and live up to it on his own responsibility. Catholicism, with its belief in the Church as the divine organization for guiding its members, confronts both the individual and the polity with fixed standards and established demands. It is, therefore, not surprising that conflicts, wherever they arise between the secular and the spiritual, the law and policy of the state and the creed and dogma of religion, tend to become more conspicuous and sometimes more violent when the more tightly organized churches are involved. In the modern world, it is Roman Catholicism and, possibly, Islam, rather than Protestantism or Buddhism or the Orthodox Church in Russia, which stand up to secularism with the coherent and unified power of a "living faith." And since the Catholic Church and the Moslem religion still have a powerful hold over the people of many countries and regions of the world, the issues in which state and religion are opposed are often most clear-cut when these two religions are involved. For example, the states where the relation between public and religiously controlled education is most difficult—France, Germany, and Italy—are just those states where Christian Democratic, i.e., primarily Catholic, parties feel deeply on this issue.

The issue of education, however, is only one among many over which state and church have been divided in modern times. There may be conflicts over the claim of secular power to participate in appointments to clerical office, in particular where the clergy, in turn, participates in civil matters like education or administering marriage contracts; over the church's claim to have the sole right to administer such contracts; or to have its view prevail in matters of family law (divorce) or criminal law (abortion, euthanasia); or to pass on, if not exercise censorship over, publications and other channels and media of communication. And it is by no means only in relation to the Catholic

Church that such conflicts may arise. Any similarly comprehensive belief system is likely to get involved in conflicts. Orthodox Judaism, for example, is represented in Israel through its own political parties which, if they were able to do so, would force their own Sabbath and dietary rules on orthodox and nonorthodox alike. So it is also with Islam in Pakistan and the Middle East, where it has or seeks predominant influence. So it is to a considerable degree with the Dutch Reformed Church in South Africa —with its rigid Calvinism and strong "elitist" and authoritarian overtones.

In understanding the issues and conflicts that may arise, however, we must distinguish among three types of situations: (1) where there is an established or an actually dominant church; (2) where there is either complete separation between church and state or where there is separation in principle and the churches have certain defined privileges; and (3) where religion faces its most powerful modern opponent, totalitarianism.

STATE RELATIONS WITH A DOMINANT CHURCH

There are still a good many states where one religion and one church are clearly accepted as dominant, and there is a close connection among the church, the government, and the general life and society of the country. This situation, of course, reflects the premodern historical relationship between church and state, in which the church, particularly through its control of education and its influence on the prevailing moral and spiritual atmosphere in the country, in effect provided the ideological foundation of the political regime. Frequently, too, the church was socially and economically interrelated with the regime either through ownership of land or because important state positions were staffed by members of the clergy. The church could then be identified with the *status quo* by both adherents and opponents of the clergy. To opponents it might become, as the French church did, Voltaire's *"l'infâme,"* an institution to be crushed by a violently anticlerical and, quite possibly, antireligious revolution. But such a revolution, on the other hand, could appear to many people as destructive of the moral foundations of a country and thus would rally against it not only the defenders of the old regime but all those fearful of atheism, laicism, and similar tendencies. As we have seen in Spain and Mexico in our own time, in such a conflict the issue of the power and influence of the church can become enmeshed with all the other great issues of ideology and politics which divide a nation.

There are many modern states in which such close ties exist. The Ethiopian Constitution of 1955, for instance, declares the Orthodox Church the established church of the state. Pakistan calls itself an "Islamic Republic." In India, the Hindu Mahasabha made a strong though unsuccessful bid to establish Hinduism as an official religious basis of the new polity. Even in Israel, Jewish law is still part of the secular code, especially in family and related matters. It is Catholicism, however, which provides perhaps the most significant case in point, in view of the large number of countries, especially in Latin America, which maintain a close connection between the state and the Catholic Church. In Colombia, for example, the Roman Catholic religion is established as "the official religion of the nation under the protection of the public powers."

Spain may serve as an illustration of the problems and difficulties which may arise under such a system. The Franco regime, actively allied with Catholicism in the

Civil War, recognized the Catholic religion as "the religion of the Spanish state [which] will be given official protection" (Article 6 of Franco's "Spaniards' Charter" of 1945), while Article 1 of the Succession Law of 1947 establishes Spain as "a Catholic, social, and representative State which . . . constitutes a Kingdom." While so far Spain is a kingdom without a king and its genuinely social and representative character may be in doubt, there can be no question about the role which the Church (together with the army and the Falange) has played as one of the three pillars of the regime. What unites Franco and the Church is above all a common fear of an anti-Franco revolution which, whether liberal, socialist, or Communist, would threaten the Church with a loss of the prerogatives it considers vital.

It is perhaps the more significant that despite this common interest and the predominant Catholicism of the Spanish people, there have been conflicts between the state and the Church. Thus Franco was unwilling to grant the full measure of the Church's claim to internal organizational autonomy; and in his Concordat with the Vatican (1953) he reserved to the state quite far-reaching rights over appointments to high clerical office. Moreover, in the contested issue of secondary education, with its system of parallel public and religious schools, the Church has had to grant the state supervision over its educational system. On the other hand, the Spanish clergy has frequently criticized some of the more reactionary policies of the political regime, in particular its suppression of labor demands and its neglect of the living conditions of the poor, since these directly challenge the social tenets of the Church. It is worth noting that failure to take note of such conditions has in the past often alienated large classes from organized religion.

SEPARATION BETWEEN STATE AND CHURCH

If issues between public power and organized religion arise even where a church is recognized as official, it is hardly surprising that they may become even more acute where such a connection no longer exists. Usually, the smallest ground for conflict exists where, as in Anglo-Saxon societies, separation prevails on the basis of mutual toleration and mutual freedom in the vital field of education. This presupposes a meeting of minds or of basic value standards—as in Britain between the general public spirit and the Anglican as well as the nonconformist creeds, and in the United States between the spirit of the public schools and that of the private, including the Catholic parochial, establishments. In the case of America, the potential gap between Christian tenets and the values of a competitive society has been bridged by a common acceptance of a set of values and ideals which are indicated in the necessarily somewhat vague term "the American way of life."

But where, as in most Continental-European countries, either disestablishment has taken place against the resistance of the churches, or where the churches, although not recognized as official, enjoy certain privileges, we encounter a continual conflict situation. The issue then tends to oppose the religious side to "laicism," which rejects all such privileges and opposes any attempt on the part of the disestablished churches to regain their former privileges. Such a conflict may result in antireligious discrimination, and churches may be deprived not only of their former privileges, but also of the rights they would customarily enjoy even under a system of complete separation. On the other hand, a grant of privileges, such as the right to control education either through a system of church-run schools or through public schools in which instruction proceeds in the spirit of the respective church, might tie the church so closely to secular authority that religion would assume an almost official character; this is especially the case where churches are subsidized from public officials. Thus, in the Protestant regions of Germany, religion has been so closely tied to the state that the pastor functioned as part of the state bureaucracy. In France, on the other hand, where "laicization" was enforced upon the religious part of the population, the antagonism of state and church perpetuates itself even to this day on the local and personal level in the relations between priest and (laicist) school teacher. In either case the issue can become one of the most profound ones dividing a nation, especially where it leads to the formation of Christian or Catholic parties or other parties whose platforms are characterized by their stand on the religious issue. Matters are made worse when the schism is accompanied by division in nationality or language groups. Thus, in Belgium, where the Flemish are more religious than the Walloon part of the population, a conflict over the education of teachers and state subsidies for the denominational school system not only involved the Social Christian Party in a struggle with the Liberal and Socialist Parties, but threatened to revive the old and bitter antagonism between the two population groups.

Wherever the law of the state decides issues in a way irreconcilable with religious tenets, individuals may find themselves in agonizing conflicts of conscience. The most obvious example is the conscientious objector who will go to prison rather than bear arms. But large-scale passive or even active resistance to the state authority may arise if national policies clash with the standards of a group which holds a nonconforming supranational creed or ideology. Democratic states are usually too tolerant and too responsive to the pressures of particular groups to permit public policy so drastically to violate individual or group consciences. But such conflicts can easily arise between religion and a totalitarian regime.

CHURCHES AND TOTALITARIAN REGIMES

In the past, churches, as one of the famous two pillars of feudal-monarchical rule—"throne and altar"—have often endorsed established social groups and conservative political forces. This made them suspect to reformers, and especially to socialists, as dispensers of "quietism" who, in Marx's phrase, purvey a spiritual opium to the ruled to keep them in an obedient frame of mind. Those who became alienated from religion for this reason often subsequently turned against churches and religion as such, especially when they themselves attained political power. The churches, in turn, tended to consider atheistic Communism their chief political enemy. When totalitarian movements rose to power under anti-Communist slogans, religious groups were therefore tempted to align themselves with these movements as allies in a common cause. This was clearest in the case of Spanish Falangism; but even in the case of Nazism, major portions of German Protestantism at first welcomed Hitler, and the Vatican concluded a Concordat with him in 1933 (as it had done earlier with Mussolini) in the hope of mutual accommodation.

Usually, however, it has not taken long to convince churches and religions that, short of sacrificing their own fundamental interests and beliefs, they cannot hope to come to terms, and even less to make common cause, with any kind of totalitarianism that takes its own ideology seriously. Both Protestantism and Catholicism ended in violent conflict with Nazism in Germany; conflict with the Church arose irrepressibly even in a Catholic country like Argentina under Peron; and as we have seen, church and state are not free from tension in Franco Spain. Religion and fascist totalitarianism (in the broader sense of the term) are incompatible, because they represent rival and total ideological claims. Even where fascism does not profess hostility to religion, it is so fundamentally wedded to ideals and principles which Christianity abhors that any real conciliation is impossible. Mussolini's ideal of bellicism and the warlike virtues, his glorification of integral nationalism as an end, and of force, violence, terror, cunning—in short, all the Machiavellian devices—as proper means, were no less pagan than Hitler's racialism and all that it involved.

Communism is no less fundamentally opposed than fascism to religious tenets, since it, too, demands the complete allegiance of its members. Thus the church-state conflict in Catholic countries under satellite rule has been inevitable. Moreover, Christian parties have been in the vanguard of anti-Communist coalitions and policies in the postwar period, and in Italy, they constitute *the* one big non-Communist party. A 1949 decree by the Congregation of the Holy Office in Rome declared that any association of a Catholic with the Communist Party, either as a member or in other ways, or through any activity in support of Communist doctrine and practice was forbidden and would incur automatic excommunication.

Can there ever be a *rapprochement* or even a *modus vivendi* between organized religion and Communism? For the foreseeable future, the prospects of an accommodation on any other basis than an uneasy truce, in which churches avoid overly harsh criticism of the regime and the regime avoids harsh persecution of the churches, seem dim indeed. But the argument has sometimes been made that while fascism is pagan, Communism is rather a "Christian heresy." This line of thought holds that the ultimate ideal of Marxian socialism, still professed by Communism, is not entirely incompatible with religious ethics: it is humanitarian and even personalistic, concerned with individuals and a better life rather than with the glory and power of nations or races, or the power of an elite or a *Fuehrer*. Soviet Communism, of course, has perverted these ideals, and the changes of the post-Stalin era hardly suggest much hope for a reversal so profound as to bring the professed ideal into compliance with actual practice. Should the unlikely happen, however, and Communism, while continuing its hold or perhaps extending it further, nevertheless forego its totalitarian features, including repressive and persecutory policies against churches and religion, the churches might then perhaps look for an accommodation which the present nature of the regime precludes. Churches have proved themselves adaptable to a wide variety of situations without sacrificing their ultimate goals; they have been able to cross the divide between continents, races, and civilizations; and they have been wont to take the long-range view, especially when the fate of many of their members was at stake. For the time being, however, their interests as well as their ideals are obviously more intimately connected with the liberal-democratic polities.

THE LIBERAL AND THE TOTALITARIAN POLITY

Thus we may expect that Communism will remain the great totalitarian challenge to religion as well as to the democracies for a long time to come. If so, the democracies will naturally ally themselves with forces and movements opposed to any form of totalitarianism: with churches and religions as long as they do not support fascist regimes or trends, and also with those governments which, while not completely democratic according to the exacting standards of the older Western democracies, yet recognize some necessary restraints and limitations upon power in order to protect individual and group rights and liberties. Some of these latter governments, because of their authoritarian heritage, have failed thus far to live up fully to all the criteria established by British or American democracy. This is still true of Germany and likewise of Japan, whose modern political developments resemble those of Germany in so many respects and whose late industrialization and strong authoritarian traditions have so far hampered genuine democratization. Not all modernized countries have been fortunate enough to enjoy the steady growth over several centuries of that incubator of liberal and democratic institutions, a rising middle class. And the newly independent non-European nations have had an even more sudden break with the past.

Recognizing the existence of such handicaps to democratic development, those nations committed to democracy can profitably draw a distinction between political democracy and liberalism and, as we have already suggested, welcome as allies in the antitotalitarian camp nations and regimes which, while more or less authoritarian in their political institutions or in their approach to decision-making, are yet liberal in the sense of respecting and protecting the dignity of the individual and the free expression of personal and group interests. As the Central European *Rechtsstaat* shows, this combination is a practicable one. In other words, where traditionalism does not exclude individual freedom and the development of personality, it may constitute a bulwark against totalitarian inroads.

In distinguishing between totalitarianism and democracy, what counts is not only the rule of the majority, but even more the right, or at least the chance, for individuals and minorities freely to develop themselves. Particularly in our mass societies, where the people at large can exercise at best only a limited control over crucial matters of domestic and foreign policy, the difference between free and totalitarian countries seems to reduce itself ultimately to one question: whether or not there exists an inviolable sphere of privacy in which the otherwise organized, mechanized, ordered, and oftentimes bullied individual may yet proceed according to his will, whim, or fantasy, his beliefs or disbeliefs, in a socially useful and adjusted or an entirely useless and unadjusted fashion. Any genuine freedom in the personal and group spheres presupposes, as we have seen, the placing of limits upon political power. It is only when there are limits on what government may do and on the way in which it may do it that citizens are free. Thus, if religion may be an ally of democracy in its conflict with totalitarianism, liberal democracy, in turn, provides the setting within which a man can most freely maintain those beliefs, religious or secular, which enhance his individuality.

VIII

THE INTERRELATIONS OF NATIONAL AND INTERNATIONAL POLITICS

No less intimately interrelated than belief systems and politics are national and international affairs. A major trend of recent times has been the growing interdependence and integration of nations in an international system where many of them become ever less independent of foreign influence. Thus, though the number of so-called independent states is rapidly increasing, all states tend in fact to be grouped into ever fewer and larger blocs. The impact of this development is increasingly reflected in the internal affairs of even the largest and most powerful states; it must therefore be analyzed with care if the study of government is to be both perceptive and genuinely comparative.

FROM SELF-SUFFICIENCY TO INTERDEPENDENCE

It is not without reason that students of comparative government have long ignored, or paid scant attention to, the impact of international affairs on national governments and politics. For some three or more centuries after the modern nation-state emerged in the late fifteenth and early sixteenth centuries, domestic affairs were relatively autonomous. Political institutions grew out of native soil, and changes, even revolutionary ones, were due to indigenous forces and indigenous movements. Foreign influences were not themselves without effect; but they were commonly transformed and shaped to fit the needs of the nation itself. Thus, liberal democracy, as we have seen, would change in coloring or even in meaning when exported from one environment to another. Indeed, throughout this period, domestic political forces and movements were less influenced by foreign affairs than themselves influences on foreign policies; as, for example, when Britain or the United States sided with liberal democratic forces or nations, or Czarist Russia backed the cause of absolutism on the Continent for its own internal political reasons.

Domestic considerations of course still influence the policies of those powers which retain a large measure of freedom in their foreign affairs. But, by and large, we have now entered a period where there is an increasing impact of world affairs on internal politics and institutions. The chief reason for the change lies in the transformation of the nation-state from a fortress into an entity incapable of assured defense against modern weapons of attack.

The essential characteristic of the modern territorial

state used to be that it was a self-contained, closed, centralized unit which could provide its citizens with protection, both in the form of internal peace and of security from outside control or interference. Fortresses lining its boundaries rendered it difficult even for stronger countries to penetrate by force of arms; and security was strengthened by alliances of weaker with stronger powers, nations' interest in the maintenance of a balance of power, and, prior to the French Revolution, a feeling among rulers that "legitimate" units as such should not be destroyed. Moreover, even when dynastic legitimacy subsequently yielded to national self-determination, the national units acquired a cohesion which made them even more integrated and permitted internal government and constitutional life to develop in accordance with the indigenous trends and inclinations of the nation's people.

By the end of the last century, however, certain developments presaged the end of this system. With industrialization, economic self-sufficiency became transformed into dependence on continued imports from abroad. World War I showed how close both Britain and Germany could come to defeat through blockade. But the decisive change has been in the nature of war. Air war, by opening the way to "vertical" invasion, has meant the end of the frontier in its traditional function of protection. Thus the basic condition which gave substance to legal sovereignty and political independence came to an end, and with it the sense of security which had enabled countries to develop their own political institutions and ways of life. To this feeling of insecurity, the possibility of a sudden, unannounced, annihilating blow by nuclear weapons adds a sense of impotence. Even the nuclear powers not only possess an overwhelming power to inflict absolute destruction on others, but, like the non-nuclear powers, are themselves equally exposed to destruction.

Few people, and even few political leaders, seem fully to have grasped the radical nature of this change from relative self-sufficiency to international interdependence. States continue in the main to act as if they were still the sovereign independent nations of the past. Despite this lack of realization, however, the effect of this transformation is reflected clearly in the emergence of "bipolarity," that is, the concentration of most of the world's power into two huge blocs through which nations attempt to gain that security which is no longer attainable within national boundaries. These blocs, of course, are led by the two superpowers, the United States and the Soviet Union, whose opposition is accentuated by the ideological conflict between democracy and Communism. Whether, through the emergence of China and possibly other states, bipolarity is about to be replaced by a system of nuclear multipolarity is a question of the—perhaps not far distant —future; but for the moment, the two superpowers are still clearly dominant.

THE IMPACT OF BIPOLARITY

Bipolarity has had two chief effects. One is that domestic issues tend to recede before foreign affairs. The other is that the leading powers and their policies have more and more influence not only on the foreign but also on the domestic affairs of other countries.

The first effect is perhaps more noticeable in democracies than in totalitarian countries. The functioning of liberal democracy has always been favored by the existence of peace, or at least of that "normalcy" in which wars were rare enough not to disturb their institutions radically and limited enough not to affect an underlying feeling of security. But since World War I in Europe, and since the end of World War II in America, too, crisis conditions in international affairs have become the normal ones; we are perennially involved in cold wars and even relieved when an outbreak of actual hostilities leads to merely localized conflict instead of the dread total war. Clearly this situation favors authoritarianism over democratic institutions; concentration of power (especially in the executive, if not the military) rather than its limitation or dispersion; broad and ill-defined mandates rather than checks and controls; and increasingly far-reaching restrictions or suspensions of individual or group rights rather than their jealous protection.

THE EFFECT OF EMERGENCIES, ACTUAL AND POTENTIAL

The bipolar split and the threat of nuclear annihilation do not, however, have the same far-reaching impact in all places and at all times. It differs in different nations and tends to change with the ups and downs in the cold war (or "cold peace") situation. For a time, the West seemed more concerned with the economic offensive of the Soviet bloc than with threats of actual hostilities. More recently, however, the threat of Soviet penetration into vital areas of Africa as well as the Middle East is again deeply ffecting American as well as Western European policies.

Such ups and downs should not deceive us into believing that, as in former ages, emergencies will come and go. The threat that nuclear war poses is a continual one, and the emergency is thus potentially always with us. We may hope that the "balance of terror"—the nuclear stalemate between the two blocs—will ensure permanent peace, but we cannot depend on it. Crises are apt to recur; and while totalitarian regimes, with their concentration of power and their absence of checks and limitations, are prepared in any case to meet crises, even where they do not provoke them, democracies, if they would try to preserve their traditional values and institutions, are confronted with grave difficulties.

These dangers were illustrated by what happened in the United States at the height of the cold war. That threats to national security may give rise to emotionalism or even to hysteria (however that loosely used term may be defined) had already been shown by the American Alien and Sedition Acts of the Napoleonic period. But the threat to traditional liberties, indeed to established constitutional life, was even greater in our nuclear and bipolar age. The power of investigation with all its connotations and effects—a power which for a while was almost unlimited and unchecked—not only affected rights and liberties (the sphere which attracted most attention), but also such constitutional principles as the separation of powers in government itself. Thus it threatened at one point to render lower and intermediate levels of the executive subject to control by members of the Congress, thereby undermining the hierarchy of the executive and the authority of its chief. And it is significant that it was neither the chief executive nor the broad public revulsion to which "McCarthyism" eventually yielded, but rather to the fact that a recession in international tension coincided with resistance on the part of smaller groups, in particular the federal judiciary and the leaders in the Protestant churches and in some universities. As for the Senator's personal power, it was a tradition-minded group among his colleagues which was chiefly responsible for its decline.

Discouraging as much of this experience was, it also

demonstrated that democracy has a resilience under stress which asserts itself sometimes in unexpected ways. Likewise, it tended to show that it is less the constitutional framework which lends or denies protection to national institutions than it is the traditions of nations and the spirit in which they and their leaders act. This can be seen still better from the way in which Western European nations reacted to the cold war situation. Thus the British, whose government had made a cautious and restrained use of legally unlimited emergency powers in both world wars, proved similarly sober in their approach to postwar problems of internal security. Instead of flooding the country with loyalty investigations and subjecting the entire civil service to identical security standards, they have applied the latter to carefully selected sensitive agencies and only to positions where spies or subversives might do real damage. More important, they never yielded to the frenzy of fear and suspicion which leads to the invasion of vital personal concerns with far-fetched charges, "faceless" accusers, and ostracism. This experience would seem to indicate that, difficult as is the problem posed to democracies by a permanent emergency in world relations, sacrifice of liberties is not inevitable.

But because McCarthyism has come and gone, we should not for this reason underestimate the less spectacular but more continual effects of potential emergencies. Americans in particular are wont to personalize politics and thus, in this instance, to consider McCarthy *the* danger (or the hero, as the case may be). But the trends are still there; so are the instruments. The Internal Security Act of 1950, for example, provides among other things for the detention in concentration camps of any suspect persons by presidential authority upon mere declaration of war.

One of the most important needs of a democracy is a

constant, unimpeded flow of information. Here, too, world tension is taking its toll. Withholding information for security reasons was intensified with the advent of "atomic secrets"; more and more government activities, moreover, are now "classified," thus limiting information all too often to prefabricated official news handouts. To some degree this is inevitable. Who among the uninitiated can judge the requirements for defense and defense establishments, and their related budgetary and other legislation? Who can judge what measures are best fitted to counter an alleged or a real aggression? But if active citizenship is not to be excluded from the fields of defense and foreign affairs, such a development means that responsible leaders have still greater need than in the past to keep the public informed not only of the reasons for such limits on information, but also of the basis on which the judgments in these fields are made.

This is no less true with respect to another effect of the nuclear age: the fact that dependence on nuclear weapons may render necessary quick decisions of a vital character. These decisions, in the ultimate case, can hardly be arrived at through prolonged democratic discussion of issues. And the ultimate decisions may be prejudiced by preceding foreign policies or, perhaps even more, by preceding military policies, which in turn may have been arrived at without genuine democratic participation or consent. Thus the procedures of democracy tend to be limited to less vital areas, and a still greater importance is placed on the responsibility of its leaders.

THE TREND TOWARD CONFORMITY

We should also notice one further effect of bipolarity: what may be called the "neutralization" of politics, the trend toward avoiding strong attitudes for or against this or that policy. Bipolarity, which implies ideological cleavage, tends to render unpopular or even unusual attitudes suspect, whether they are held by individuals or by groups. This has always been a characteristic of totalitarianism, where the essence of control consists in the suppression of deviating opinion. But it is becoming noticeable in non-totalitarian countries also. The very existence of a totalitarian opponent tends to render dissent suspect and thus to encourage conformity. But, strangely, such conformity does not reject what Communism, where it is in actual control, stands for: authoritarianism, rigidity, deprivation of liberty. On the contrary, conformity opposes what Communism itself destroys: espousal of reform, protection of rights, safeguarding of liberties. This renders the less stout citizen timid; for fear of being tainted red he tries hard to appear colorless and to avoid the controversial. While in the nineteenth century broad movements for change and reform in the major nations were often backed by large popular majorities, today most of the people in some of the same countries are either politically apathetic or conservative (if not reactionary). While in the last century young people, and especially university students, were in the forefront of reform, today it is rather the small elite groups which retain interest in the great political issues. Samuel Stouffer's study of *Communism, Conformity, and Civil Liberties* has revealed how small a percentage of the average people in the United States, for instance, stands for protection of civil liberties; and in Germany, the flight into political neutrality characterizes even groups which, like labor, used to be in the forefront of political action.

Other factors besides bipolarization have helped to create this trend toward conformity. The making of vital decisions without the participation of the public, which lacks the necessary information for reasons we have noted, cannot help but create political indifference. There is the impact of the mass media of communication, which tend to devote less and less time and effort to political matters, and, when they do handle them, tend to be conservative or else colorless. Lastly, the rising living standard and improved social services in countries like the United States and Britain, by wiping out a good deal of the former inequality in wealth or status, have rendered the masses of the people so satisfied that their interest in class or other social and economic issues has declined.

On the other hand, it is in countries and regions like Latin America, the Middle East, the Far East, or Southeast Asia that the political involvement and concern which we characterized as typical of the nineteenth century still prevail. It is noteworthy that it is in just these areas that student involvement in politics is still common, as witness the role of students in the 1960 overthrow of regimes in Turkey as well as in Korea.

We thus arrive at the somewhat paradoxical conclusion that although grinding poverty, economic anxiety, or class division render the functioning of genuine democracy difficult, the very solution of these problems likewise involves difficulties to democracy. Can a society which has reached a high level of material satisfactions generate that continual concern with civic issues that is at the root of active democracy? Can it do so particularly in times when concern with domestic matters is bound periodically to recede behind apprehensions about the international situation?

RELATIONS BETWEEN STRONGER AND LESSER POWERS

Let us now turn to the other impact of the new power system in the world, that of the "superpowers" on lesser states and, in particular, on their allies. There is nothing new in unequal relationships between stronger and weaker powers. They have, in the past, accounted for dependencies of all sorts, ranging all the way from mere strategic or economic influences to protectorate or colonial relationships. But except in the latter case, when the dominant power assumes complete control, domestic affairs have usually stayed within the autonomous control of the weaker power. The contrast today is that similar relations affect to a much greater degree the internal policies and systems of the dependent units. This does not mean that such dependency automatically involves control over the details of day-to-day policy-making. But it may well affect a nation's fundamental decisions about social and economic structure, political constitutions and freedoms, and similar basic issues, which used to be settled through the actions of national parties or movements within the framework of national institutions and processes.

The issue of internal Communism is the most striking example of this trend. The Communist Party is still legal and still strong in France and in Italy. But it is practically excluded from official positions in government coalitions. This is because internal alignments in our days are liable to have foreign-policy connotations. As long as Italy is in NATO, for instance, can one visualize Communist participation in a government through which Communist ministers might share the secrets of a military alliance? The Communist Party, as ex-Premier Mollet has put it, is "neither Left nor Right, but East."

In the East, of course, anything other than Communism is excluded. But, increasingly, Western democratic states also use their influence to ensure what might be called the stability, "political health," or reliability of an ally. What happened in Athens at the time of "liberation" (as reported by Churchill) differed little even in detail from what happened at the same time in Bucharest. Thereafter, the United States twice interfered in Greece in order to influence a change in its electoral system, not because it feared that the existing system might result in the victory of what was, in any case, an outlawed Communist Party, but in order to enhance the chances of a group of parties believed to be more favorably inclined to the West than was another group. There was open use of American influence on behalf of the Christian Democrats at the time of the Italian election of 1953. In the same year, American backing of Adenauer and his Christian Democrats in West Germany was not without effect on his victory over the Social Democrats, who were likewise Western-oriented but somewhat neutralist. The possibility of an "agonizing reappraisal" of American policy was made known to a France hesitant to integrate itself with Europe, and particularly with Western Germany. At that time, a French journalist was said to have declared that he would now take out American citizenship papers so as to be able to exercise some influence on French affairs!

On the other hand, attempts to influence or to control too closely or too rudely the affairs of less powerful countries are apt to backfire. Even Soviet control, which in contrast to Western influence is exercised primarily through Red Army and Communist Party control of local governments, faces the danger of "nationalist deviation." In the West, the issue of Western orientation may tend either to make any but the alliance orientation appear subversive and thus compel all major groups and parties to agree basically on one and the same foreign policy; or it may tend to split all or most of the existing groups and parties over this issue. In the latter event, a Western orientation may raise more political and general antagonism than it is worth militarily; it may even lead, as in Iceland, to the threatened denunciation of arrangements for the stationing of troops. This will then confront the "occupying" power with the choice of trying to hold on by force or of yielding to circumstances.

Such foreign- or military-policy issues tend in many of the lesser powers to overshadow what used to be considered the most vital domestic issues: those of socialism, the welfare state, or free enterprise. Thus, whereas parties and movements were seldom divided primarily over foreign affairs in the past, these issues now have so great an impact on the lesser powers that questions like neutralism vs. alignment with a super-power, the granting of bases to a foreign power, colonialism, imperialism, and the like often preoccupy their minds and policies to the exclusion, or at least the detriment, of internal issues. This cannot but have its effect on traditional party systems and policies. With the exception of the Communist Party and, to a lesser extent, the MRP *(Mouvement Républicain Populaire)*, there was not a single French party which was not split about equally over the issue of the European Defense Community. In West Germany, the effect was at first the opposite—one of leading almost every party to agree on the basic, that is, the Western foreign-policy orientation. In Britain, the two great parties are basically bipartisan in foreign issues (their sharp differences over British military action during the Suez crisis were almost without precedent), so that where there is some opposition to current foreign policy, as, for example, in the form of neutralism, or over the question of nuclear armaments, it cuts into a particular party, such as the Labour Party, and weakens it from within. Thus the international situation influences the relations, alignments, and strength of those political forces within nations which used to be guided primarily by domestic issues.

THE MAJOR POWERS AND THE "UNCOMMITTED" WORLD

Lastly, we may ask how bipolarity with its ascendancy of the superpowers affects those nations which so far have avoided close alignment with either bloc, and in this sense are uncommitted. For the most part, the latter belong to the category of "backward" or underdeveloped countries. Many of them are newly independent and thus faced with the problems of establishing their own political and constitutional systems and procedures. In many of them, such as India, Pakistan, Ceylon, or the Philippines, previous Western influence and control have determined their present governmental institutions and political processes at least in a formal way. Western-type parliamentary systems, parties, and elections abound; and occasionally the experience of these nations has added significantly to our knowledge of democratic possibilities, as when elections held in still largely illiterate India and Ghana demonstrate that literacy is no indispensable requirement for genuine expression of the popular will. Whether or not these countries become or remain genuine democracies depends, however, both on their own evolving traditions and on the influence and example of the major powers.

Let us consider for a moment some of the pulls and counterpulls which operate on such underdeveloped but steadily advancing states. Since they have only recently evolved from colonial status and have done so mainly as the result of nationalist movements which demanded independence, these states are vigorously anticolonial in attitude. The very fact that the powers from which they gained their independence were Western ones can provide a natural bias against the latter, which is not difficult for the Soviet Union and China to exploit. Moreover, because Western countries have a relatively high standard of living, their experience may well seem to have less relevance to underdeveloped countries than that of a country like the Soviet Union or China, which so recently was in a condition like their own.

It would be a mistake to underestimate, however, the attraction of the liberal democratic ideal to some of these newly emancipated states. It may well be true that to the great mass of their people it is more important to escape from their grinding poverty than to secure personal liberties. But even the most poverty-stricken person has a sense of his own personal dignity for which he desires respect. Even at this level the right to protest and to propose is a cherished one. But more important in shaping the immediate destinies of states like India and Nigeria is the fact that their leaders have a keen feeling for democratic values and are attempting courageously in the face of great difficulties to put them into operation in their societies.

Seen in this context, it is not what the Western democracies say in the way of propaganda that will be decisive for their influence in the uncommitted countries, but what they do. The action (or inaction) of the Western powers will be significant on two quite different levels. In the first place, it is obvious that their activities can have a great impact when they answer the basic needs of these countries. There are two ways in which the underdeveloped nations can modernize and industrialize: through their own unaided efforts but at the cost of totalitarian controls such as those of the Soviet Union or Communist China; or with assistance from outside. If it can be shown that Western economic and technical assistance will aid their development to such a degree that they can both industrialize and retain their Western-type institutions and freedoms, these institutions may gain the mass backing which is essential for their continued survival. In the competitive struggle with the Soviet Union for the good will of these states, it will be far more important to provide this opportunity for democratic institutions to root themselves in popular favor than to achieve any immediate backing on a particular issue.

Not only is it important to provide the kind of economic aid which can underpin democratic regimes; it is also vital for Western states to honor those who struggle to keep them in operation. In this respect, all too little has been done. American ties with Franco Spain can presumably be justified on strategic grounds; but until all too recently, Trujillo's dictatorship seemed to have received about as much support as its more democratically deserving neighbors. President Jiménez of Venezuela was officially honored in Washington, whereas no similar honor had been conferred on representatives of the preceding democratic regime in that country. When such actions are contrasted with the open American opposition to the leftist (though by no means entirely Communist-controlled) government in Guatemala, which contributed greatly to its overthrow in 1954, uncommitted countries may well come to feel that the major Western democratic powers are opposed to only one among many types of nondemocratic governments.

To support democratic forces in the underdeveloped countries may well be the most, perhaps even the only, effective way to counter potentially strong Soviet or other Communist influence. In its recent policies, the Soviet Union has combined the appeal to indigenous nationalism —the strongest political and ideological force in those areas —with attempts to satisfy these countries' basic material needs through economic aid. In certain respects, its attitude toward these countries has been more "democratic" than that of the democratic states themselves. Thus the Soviet Union has ostentatiously maintained that there are no political strings attached to its economic aid. Moreover, its studied efforts at correctness in its relations with the underdeveloped countries sometimes arouse less suspicion than do those of Western countries which still retain vestiges of their traditional attitudes of superiority.

Effective influence on the new states thus also requires a second type of action on the part of Western states: a convincing demonstration that they are truly democratic in actions as well as words. Having long lived under foreign domination and discrimination, the underdeveloped countries (or at least their leaders) care as greatly about being treated on a basis of equality and respect as about improving their material conditions. A major reason why the newer countries of the Commonwealth of Nations—India, Pakistan, Ceylon, Ghana, Nigeria, and Malaya—prize their membership is because, in addition to receiving material advantages, they are treated as equals in that association. To the extent that the West actually practices democratic virtues both in its relations with the new states and at home, it enjoys a vast advantage over its totalitarian opponents, whose words are contradicted by realities, particularly with regard to domestic practices. The degree to which democratic values, especially equality (including racial equality) and personal and group liberties, are demonstrable may, in fact, determine in large measure what direction the so-called uncommitted nations will take. Thus the practice of democracy in countries like Great Britain and the United States may turn out to be decisive for the ultimate fate of freedom throughout the world.

THE IMPACT OF INTERNATIONAL ORGANIZATION

We have spoken of the tremendous changes which have transformed a world of self-sufficient and separate nations into an ever more integrated whole within which all nations tend to become interdependent. Population trends and pressures affect not only particular nations, but, with their by-products of migration and (in extreme cases) of refugee and expellee groups and stateless persons, all the other countries, too. The "population explosion" as such (coupled with the exhaustion of vital natural resources and the problem of lagging food supplies in large parts of the world) poses almost as great a world problem today as security from aggression and nuclear annihilation. And as far as the latter is concerned, certainly no more urgent task can be imagined than that of providing for effective collective security or other international devices to protect the world from utter destruction.

And, indeed, there has been no lack of efforts along these lines. For the last hundred years there have been attempts to bring about the closer integration of sovereign nations through the establishment of agencies for the pursuit of common purposes. This trend culminated in the League of Nations system and that of its successor, the United Nations, with its many affiliated agencies in economic, cultural, and humanitarian fields. A vast number of activities are now coordinated or carried on through these channels.

The effect of these developments, however, can be interpreted in two very different ways, depending on one's ultimate objective. To those who believe that the effectiveness of international organization depends on the actual transfer of functions and powers now in the domain of sovereign nations—whether in the fields mentioned above or of security against war and aggression—the progress which has been made is very small. These people would claim that an effective solution of the world-wide problems of resources or of migration requires a transfer of genuine lawmaking powers to a supranational body which would have the power to supervise the implementation of policies and the administration of programs initiated by national agencies. Genuine collective security, in this view, requires the abdication by member nations of discretion over their power to direct military policies and to make war.

It is clear that despite their exposure to the nuclear danger and their inability independently to solve other world problems, nations have been unwilling to make these transfers of jurisdiction and renunciation of power. Whatever they have been doing by way of international cooperation has been (as the term indicates) voluntary and based on calculations of the national interest. But this is not to say that their interpretation of their vital interests has not led nations to make increasing use of international organization for purposes which are both to their advantage and beyond their own scope. One of the most obvious places where this has happened is in activities which concern refugees: not only in the vast numbers of such homeless people dealt with by the International Refugee Organization through its camps, shipping facilities, and migration service, but also in such sudden emergencies as the one created by the outflow of refugees after the abortive Hungarian revolt against Soviet control late in 1956, and in the results achieved through World Refugee Year. In fields like health, food and agriculture, and technical assistance, international organization is being used to facilitate activities which no one country can adequately undertake by its own efforts. Most spectacular, and ultimately most significant, may be the international forces which maintain the peace between Israel and the Arab states, and within the Congo.

It would also be a mistake to underestimate the moral influence of the United Nations. This affects the policies of states both by example and by expectation. The newer countries have learned much about the practices of more mature ones through contact in United Nations organizations. The principle of equality for women and the Declaration of Human Rights may not be accepted fully in some Latin-American and Asian countries which call themselves democratic, but it is more difficult for these countries to withstand pressures at home to extend such rights when they have been promoted on the international level. It is worth remembering that the outcry against slavery in Liberia arose after World War I in the League of Nations and led to the stamping out of the practice. Even when nations find justification in traditional standards of self-interest for interfering forcibly in a national situation, as Great Britain and France did in the Suez crisis late in 1956, the protests in the United Nations (and indeed among the British people themselves) indicated new and widespread assumptions about the use of United Nations channels which can hardly help having an influence on future national policies. Even the Soviet Union, with its rigorous insistence on its right to interfere in the Hungarian revolt and with its vast military strength, had to stand a fire of criticism and moral reprobation from smaller countries, while its efforts to make capital out of the Congo crisis in mid-1960 were largely thwarted through the support of United Nations action by independent African states. In a world where major power blocs strive for the support of the uncommitted countries, debates on the platform of the United Nations are far from being without influence.

For the foreseeable future, it is along these lines that international organization seems likely to have its greatest effect. It is true that here and there, and in a preparatory way, as it were, steps have been taken which might facilitate the working of genuine international organization, or even international government, if ever the world should become ready for it. Thus some postwar constitutions, notably those of France and West Germany, and postwar amendments to some older constitutions, notably in the case of Holland and Denmark, provide for a possible transfer of legislative, administrative, and judicial authority to an international organization or organizations. Both the Ghanaian and the Guinean Constitutions include similar provisions for possible transfer of authority to a larger Pan-African state. A postwar British statute goes so far as to provide that Security Council decisions with binding force on member states shall be directly binding on British subjects. But the practical significance of the constitutional provisions we have mentioned has not been in relation to international organization in general, but rather with respect to certain regional organizations that have arisen in the postwar period, particularly in Western Europe, such as the European Coal and Steel Community, Euratom, and the Common Market.

These examples show that at least some nations under certain circumstances are willing to sacrifice their previous rights and to engage in thus far untried and novel ventures. The fact that what success there has been is along regional rather than world-wide lines indicates the importance of building on common interests and common understanding. The growing speed with which the West European integration movement is developing underscores the value of the vast amount of patient negotiation and detailed planning which goes into such endeavors.

So long, however, as nations seek salvation in blocs and similar agglomerations, that is, in the concentration rather than the transfer of power, there is acute danger for all countries in a world of nations which are split ideologically and armed with weapons of destruction. It may be optimistic, but perhaps not utopian, to expect that this realization of both common dangers and common objectives will in the end prove stronger than the pull of fear and the urge toward power. In that event, international organization will have an impact on government and politics far greater than any other force in the world today.

IX

DEMOCRACY IN THE MODERN WORLD

Now that we have concluded this survey of some of the forces and problems which confront governments today, we are ready to return to two basic questions of central interest in this book: What is the essential nature of democracy and of dictatorship? And how valid are the charges against democracy which were raised in the beginning of this book? In reaching our final conclusions on these matters, we must keep in mind that there are many states with a greater or lesser leaning toward democracy which are neither completely democratic nor dictatorial; that democracies are subject to strains of emotion, fear, and self-interest which sometimes lead them to adopt techniques or, temporarily, even objectives more characteristic of dictatorships than they like to realize; and that in the world of today both the tasks and the organization of government are at all times complex, highly demanding, and absolutely vital to the future of the political community.

THE TWO PATTERNS OF DEMOCRACY AND DICTATORSHIP

Despite the strains and tensions to which democracies are subject, there remain certain clear differentiations between democracy and dictatorship which are worth reiterating. As we have seen, in a totalitarian dictatorship the power exercised by its governing group is unlimited and unrestrained, and the authority of the regime extends into every aspect of the life of the individual. In a democracy, the exercise of political power is limited by a constitutional framework which protects certain areas of life from governmental interference and provides that the powers allowed the government shall be exercised according to known rules and procedures. The simplest distinction to be made between these two forms of government is thus between unlimited and limited government. As a wit has said, "In democracies what is not forbidden is permitted; in dictatorships it is compulsory."

Behind these differences lie two sharply contrasting conceptions of the political community. The first, endorsed by both the Soviet and Nazi dictatorships, is that this community is an entity with a particular purpose of its own, which may be something quite different from the immediate purposes and desires of its members. This view is linked in turn to a belief in historical inevitability. Thus, the Soviet leaders, accepting the materialist conception of history, determine policy in the light of this (supposed) key to the future. In classical Marxism, of course, the state was stigmatized as an instrument of oppression used by the ruling class; Lenin envisioned it as an instrument of the working class in freeing itself from its oppressors. Stalin maintained that the Soviet state is a necessary protection of the working class against capitalist encirclement; and his successors continue to agree that it is the instrument for building the socialist society, which history (at least Marxist history) proves is the form of organization most in accord with advanced modes of economic production.

National Socialism similarly had its *Weltanschauung,* or world view, from which could be deduced the course of history. Its emphasis was on racialism, in contrast to the Marxist stress on economic determinism. But in the general view that the purposes of the organized political community are far superior to those of the individuals who compose it, there is little difference between fascism and Marxism. Consequently, they both deny that there should be any limit on the exercise of political power on behalf of such a community.

Democracy does not deny that there may be meaning in history, but its advocates insist that there is no *one* meaning, and that there is no inevitability in history—because they believe men have the opportunity to shape their own future within the limits provided by their experience and their environment. Thus, the advocates of democracy point out that Marx's prophecies about the inevitable collapse of capitalism failed to materialize because, for one thing, people were forewarned by his prophecy and proceeded to take measures against the widening division between labor and capital that was taking place in his time. Instead of believing that the future is already determined by the conditions of the present, democratic thinkers maintain that man can use his intelligence to direct policies so as to modify, if not forestall, what may seem to be impending.

But if man can so act, it is a natural corollary that the state is controlled by individuals, and not that the state gives meaning to the lives of individuals. And at this point we return to the conception of limits which has been put forward as the characteristic feature of a democracy. For it is only when there are limits on what the government may do, and on the way in which it may do it, that the citizens are in control. In a mass society, the controls should ultimately be in the hands of the whole community, but within such a framework of limitations that the rights of individuals and of minorities are protected.

It is apparent that this definition of "liberal" democracy is far different from the "plebiscitary" democracy which the French Revolution may have seemed to preach. It implies that democracy is more than the rule of the majority. It suggests that the right of the individual to pursue his own spiritual and cultural life and the right of minorities to express their views freely and to influence policy are as much a part of democracy as popular control. It is for this reason that countries like Great Britain and France as well as the United States cherish civil liberties and that the opposition plays so vital a part in the British parliamentary process.

It has often been said, however, that only countries reared in a tradition of constitutionalism have respect for such limitations upon government. Nor can we deny that the countries in which Marxism and fascism have had the greatest effect are those which most lacked a constitutional tradition. Thus it seems clear that newly independent countries like India have a great initial handicap in establishing limited political democracy because of the slightness of their earlier constitutional tradition (and even India knows much more about constitutionalism because of its long contact with the British than do many other politically new countries). And yet, if the earlier argument has been correct, the essential requirement of democracy in these new countries, as in the older democracies, will be the acceptance of restraints on the operations of government and the willingness to follow empirical methods rather than an unrestrained rule that operates in terms of some preconceived goal.

It is, however, necessary to be realistic about what is expected of a state under modern conditions. Beyond the traditional democratic demands of civil and political rights are the hopes and expectations encouraged by the material achievements of science and industrial technology. As scientific knowledge expands, so does the sphere of political activity. Whatever is capable of organization and manipulation will ultimately come, to some degree at least, within the state's purview. All the more reason, therefore, to confront the actualities of politics and world affairs with the experimental spirit of science. While Soviet leaders are hampered by a doctrinaire Marxism, the students and practitioners of politics in democratic states can be constantly searching for new ways to meet their problems, borrowing from others where it fits their needs and countering the dangers with which they are constantly confronted.

CAN DEMOCRACY WORK?

The charges against democracy raised at the beginning, it may be remembered, were of two types. First are those that concern the machinery of democratic government—the instruments of information, the party system, representative institutions, and the making and administering of policy. But there are also questions that probe somewhat more deeply and raise the issue of whether the mental and moral qualities necessary for the successful functioning of democracy are not lacking under modern conditions; whether the enormously increased responsibilities of government are not too numerous and complex for the comprehension of the ordinary citizen; and whether the conditions of economic strain, international conflict, and class hostility have not destroyed the reasonableness, patience, and tolerance necessary for voluntary peaceful agreement.

THE MACHINERY OF DEMOCRACY EVALUATED

When we look at those questions which concern the machinery of democratic governments and then reconsider the vast variety of institutional forms which exist, we realize that there is no such thing as a "democratic political machinery" in general. On the contrary, one of the greatest strengths of democracy is the abundant variety of devices and combinations of devices which can be used to achieve free, representative, responsible, and efficient government. There may be a two-party system or a multi-party system or even a more or less democratic one-party system; the parties themselves may be highly disciplined, loosely disciplined, or not disciplined at all—and the same party system may include several kinds of parties. Authority may be divided among the legislature, the cabinet, the party organizations, the civil service, or even extra-governmental groups in any number of possible combinations. The cabinet may be composed of one party or several, or even, as in the curious situation in Austria, of both major parties on a cartel-like basis of "parity." The legislature may have a clear party majority or a system which prevents any party from getting a majority. It may be elected in a great variety of ways, from the simple direct election of the House of Commons to the indirect election of the French Council of the Republic. There can be such anachronisms as the hereditary House of Lords, or the appointive system under which the Canadian Senate has traditionally operated. The legislature may have a set of specialized committees or a number of them which are unspecialized, and it may arrange its procedure so that ministers or high officials dominate the proceedings or so that private members assume the leadership. The government may administer a large number of public services directly, or it may use devices like the public corporation. Different degrees of authority may be given to civil servants, who may be recruited in a variety of ways and with a variety of qualifications in mind. There is no necessary uniformity in the pattern of local government or in the division of authority between national and local governments, or, where there is a federal structure, between the federation and its components. Even the courts may follow the most divergent patterns of organization and training. No single formula is obligatory. The very lack of authoritarianism in principle encourages experiment and inventiveness.

Every country necessarily develops its own type of political institutions in terms of its historical heritage, its social and economic institutions, and its ultimate objectives. Moreover, these political institutions have their own coherence or inner logic. Thus a powerful legislative committee system is not compatible with the strong executive of the British parliamentary system, which works through its control of the House of Commons, while it is compatible with the powerful American executive, because the latter has its separate sphere of action. In other words, no particular means of political action or political control can be judged apart from its context. Moreover, no failure of one set of democratic institutions on the mechanical level can be taken as proof of the failure of democratic machinery in general.

At the same time, there are certain tests by which we can determine the health of a democracy. Is its constitutional framework of individual rights and recognized procedures jealously safeguarded? Are its press and other channels of expression presenting full and accurate information, providing a channel for the expression of all important political ideas, and promoting the discussion which is essential for popular participation in politics? Do its channels of political action operate to facilitate criticism, to enable minorities to differ from the majority and to make their views heard with ease within parties, parliament, and the country at large, and to ensure that at intervals the general policy of a government is passed upon by the voters in a general election? And is power, whether centered in political leaders, or parliaments, or a particular party, or even a particular group within the country, being exercised responsibly in the interests of the common good? In any nation in which some of these questions must be answered in the negative, one may seriously question whether democratic government can long endure.

THE ASSUMPTION OF DEMOCRACY EVALUATED

Underlying these tests of the working of a democratic system are certain assumptions about human beings which do not go unchallenged. Many have questioned the capacity of people to understand the voluminous and technical problems of modern government; others suggested that war and economic strife have destroyed the qualities of character needed for peaceful agreement and compromise. It is clear that no governmental device can make men more intelligent or public-spirited or tolerant or reasonable than their own capacity and the conditions of modern life permit. The fundamental question for democracy today is whether, however adequate the machinery, human beings have the qualities of mind and character to make it function.

Fortunately, the attack on the capacities and character of the ordinary citizen is overly simple in some of its assumptions. The citizen does not have to be technically competent in every phase of governmental activity in order to judge whether or not he is well-governed. The political decisions required of him are relatively simple, and he is not ill-equipped to make them. As Aristotle noted, the person who eats a dinner is as good a judge of its quality as the cook. The citizen is concerned with purposes and results rather than the technical means of accomplishing them. It requires a technician to plan and build a bridge, but it is the citizen who knows better than anyone else his own desires and needs, and he is better equipped than anyone else to tell whether his government is satisfying them.

The Western democracies have provided us with considerable evidence that an educated and experienced electorate is not a bad judge of the important issues of modern politics. So have some of the newer Asian and African states like India, the Philippines, Nigeria, and the Ivory Coast. Certainly those prophets who expected the extension of the suffrage to result in a tide of reckless and revolutionary legislation have been badly disappointed. Even in foreign relations, where the judgment of the ordinary citizen would seem most badly handicapped by lack of personal knowledge and experience, the policy of the older and newer democracies has never been so disastrous as that of a Hitler or a Mussolini; and there is some reason for believing that the leaders of the Soviet Union, despite their reputation for Machiavellian cunning, have not been more accurate in their assessment of political realities than have democratic statesmen—and have made as many blunders, if not more.

In fact, a survey of modern governments suggests that some of those observers who have been most ruthless in their assessment of the political incapacity of the people have been most credulous in their willingness to attribute supernatural qualities of wisdom and integrity to the leaders and administrators of authoritarian states. Yet, revelations of the nature of Hitler and his "court" disclose a degree of folly of which no democracy has shown itself capable. Similarly, it would be hard to think of a more devastating indictment of Soviet leadership than the revelations about Stalin made by the Soviet's own top leadership.

If one turns from the question of technical competence to that of the moral preconditions for successful democratic government—calmness, reasonableness, and patience in arriving at decisions; a desire to come to peaceful agreement and, therefore, a willingness to make concessions and compromises; a feeling of confidence that no political group will attempt to impose its will by force, or use violent means to keep other groups from attaining power, or overthrow the constitutional system—it seems clear that such qualities are not easily and quickly acquired, but rather are fostered by long experience and, in general, by favorable economic, social, and even geographical circumstances. Where such qualities and experience are lacking, democracy is, at best, difficult to establish; it is significant that in countries like Great Britain and the

Democracy in the Modern World

United States, where democracy has been most successful, children are taught from their earliest schooldays to play the game, accept defeat with good sportsmanship and victory with generosity, abide by the will of the majority, and take criticism and disagreement in good part. In fact, the very success with which these qualities are inculcated in the democracies—the belief that any problem can be solved if only men of good will meet each other in reasonable discussion around a table—has made it difficult for their leaders to understand and deal with those representatives of authoritarian governments who, like Hitler before World War II or the Soviet leaders today, cannot think in terms of enduring compromise but only in terms of total victory and crushing defeat; who regard concessions as a sign of weakness and a compromise not as an enduring agreement but rather as a resting place on the road to the complete achievement of their original aims; who look forward to crushing their enemies, and who cannot conceive of tolerating a "loyal opposition."

More than education is necessary for the cultivation of the political attitudes required for democratic government. In general, democracy flourishes best where there is a feeling of security and of economic well-being. The man who suffers from grinding poverty and the anxieties of unemployment finds it difficult to be reasonable and detached in his judgments, to weigh judiciously the fate of the commonwealth while ignoring the hunger of his children. The person who lives under conditions of civil strife is all too likely to consider order, even when brought about by a strong man, preferable to the uncertainty and danger of a freer existence. And yet peoples with a satisfying philosophy, be it Christian, Buddhist, or Hindu, may well rise above the strains of everyday life to retain their faith in the values of freedom. Few recent experiences have been more startling or, in a sense, encouraging, than to find how strongly the Hungarian people retained their desire for freedom despite the rigorous rule and indoctrination of one of the most highly organized of Soviet satellites. Nor should we underestimate the desire for human dignity and racial equality on the part of the people of color who have recently emerged or are emerging to nationhood.

The democratic way of political life is not an easy one, but its rewards are great. No form of government is simpler than that of one man ruling over others; yet all history stands as a record of the abuse of power so concentrated. Democracy requires from its citizens a level of political intelligence, experience, maturity, public spirit, and self-restraint which is lacking in large parts of the world; and it also demands the exercise of ingenuity in finding solutions and developing the political machinery appropriate for a system which desires freedom and responsibility as well as efficiency. The great strength of democracy is that its way of life fosters and encourages these very qualities. It is in the democracies that no one attitude or solution is orthodox, that diversity and experiment are considered natural and desirable. And as one looks at the great variety of devices which have in practice been developed for the realization of democratic aims, it would be rash to conclude that in imaginativeness, willingness to experiment, and social idealism, the democracies yield in any way to other forms of government.

SELECTED BIBLIOGRAPHY

ALMOND, GABRIEL A., et al. *The Appeals of Communism.* Princeton, N. J.: Princeton University Press; London: Oxford University Press, 1955.

———, and Coleman, James S. (eds.). *The Politics of the Developing Areas.* Princeton, N. J.: Princeton University Press, 1960.

ARENDT, HANNAH, *The Origins of Totalitarianism* (2nd enl. ed.). New York: Meridian Books, 1958.

BOWIE, ROBERT R., and FRIEDRICH, CARL J. *Studies in Federalism.* Boston: Little, Brown & Co., 1954.

BRIMMEL, J. H. *Communism in South East Asia: A Political Analysis.* London and New York: Oxford University Press for the Royal Institute of International Affairs, 1959.

BROGAN, D. W. *Citizenship Today: England—France—the United States.* Chapel Hill, N. C.: University of North Carolina Press, 1960.

BRYCE, VISCOUNT JAMES. *Modern Democracies.* 2 vols. London and New York: The Macmillan Co., 1924.

CARTER, GWENDOLEN M. *Independence for Africa.* New York: Frederick A. Praeger; London: Thames and Hudson, 1960.

CHAMBERS, WILLIAM N., and SALISBURY, ROBERT H. (eds.). *Democracy in the Mid-Twentieth Century, Problems and Prospects.* St. Louis, Mo.: Washington University Press, 1960.

CHAPMAN, BRIAN. *The Profession of Government. The Public Service in Europe.* New York: The Macmillan Co.; London: Allen & Unwin, 1959.

DUVERGER, MAURICE. *Political Parties: Their Organization and Activity in the Modern State.* Translated by BARBARA AND ROBERT NORTH. New York: John Wiley & Sons; London: Methuen & Co., 1954.

EHRMANN, HENRY W. (ed.). *Interest Groups on Four Continents.* Pittsburgh, Pa.: University of Pittsburgh Press, 1958.

FINER, HERMAN. *The Theory and Practice of Modern Government.* New York: Henry Holt & Co.; London: Methuen & Co., 1949.

FRIEDMAN, W. (ed.). *The Public Corporation: A Comparative Symposium.* Toronto: Carswell Company; London: Stevens & Sons, 1954.

FRIEDRICH, CARL J. *Constitutional Government and Democracy; Theory and Practice in Europe and America* (rev. ed.). Boston: Ginn & Company, 1960.

———, and BRZEZINSKI, ZBIGNIEW K. *Totalitarian Dictatorship and Autocracy.* Boston: Harvard University Press; London: Oxford University Press, 1954.

—— (ed.). *Totalitarianism*. Boston: Harvard University Press; London: Oxford University Press, 1954.

HECKSCHER, GUNNAR. *The Study of Comparative Government and Politics*. New York: The Macmillan Co., 1957.

HERZ, JOHN H. *International Politics in the Atomic Age*. New York: Columbia University Press; London: Oxford University Press, 1959.

——. *Political Realism and Political Idealism*. Chicago: University of Chicago Press; London: Cambridge University Press, 1951.

IPI SURVEY. *The Press in Authoritarian Countries*. Zurich: The International Press Institute, 1959.

KONVITZ, MILTON R., and ROSSITER, CLINTON (eds.). *Aspects of Liberty: Essays Presented to Robert E. Cushman*. Ithaca, N. Y.: Cornell University Press; London: Oxford University Press, 1959.

LOEWENSTEIN, KARL. *Political Power and the Governmental Process*. Chicago: University of Chicago Press; London: Cambridge University Press, 1957.

MACRIDIS, ROY C. (ed.). *Foreign Policy in World Politics*. Englewood Cliffs, N. J.: Prentice-Hall, 1958.

MARX, FRITZ MORSTEIN. *The Administrative State: An Introduction to Bureaucracy*. Chicago: University of Chicago Press; London: Cambridge University Press, 1958.

MYRDAL, GUNNAR. *Beyond the Welfare State: Economic Planning and its International Implications*. New Haven, Conn.: Yale University Press, 1960.

NEUMANN, SIGMUND (ed.). Modern Political Parties. *Approaches to Comparative Politics*. Chicago: University of Chicago Press; London: Oxford University Press, 1956.

ROSSITER, CLINTON LAWRENCE. *Constitutional Dictatorship: Crisis Government in the Modern Democracies*. Princeton, N. J.: Princeton University Press; London: Oxford University Press, 1948.

SPIRO, HERBERT J. *Government by Constitution*. New York: Random House, 1959.

VERNEY, D. V. *The Analysis of Political Systems*. London: Routledge & Kegan Paul, 1959.

What Are the Problems of Parliamentary Government in West Africa? London: The Hansard Society of Parliamentary Government, 1958.

WHEARE, KENNETH C. *Federal Government* (3rd ed.). London: Oxford University Press, 1954.

——. *Modern Constitutions*. London: Oxford University Press, 1951.